Environment and Sustainable Development

Indo-Canadian Perspectives

Environment and Sustainable Development

Indo-Canadian Perspectives

Edited by

Professor K.R.G. Nair

Director, Centre for Canadian Studies University of Delhi

Professor G.S. Roonwal

Director, Centre for Geo-Resources University of Delhi

Dr. Yamini Gupt

Faculty Member, Department of Business Ecomomics, University of Delhi

Foreword by

Mr. Roger Finan

Regional Director

International Development Research Centre

South Asian Regional Office, New Delhi

Kaveri Books

New Delhi - 110 002

First Published in 2002
Second Impression 2025

ISBN-10: 81-7479-058-6
ISBN-13: 978-81-7479-058-3

Published by
Kaveri Books
4832/24, Ansari Road
New Delhi-110002 (India)
Tel: 011-23288140, 4707 2321
E-mail : info@kaveribooks.com
kaveribooks@gmail.com
Website: www.kaveribooks.com

PRINTED IN INDIA

Acknowledgements

A multidisciplinary volume with 14 contributions from almost as many disciplines cannot see the light of day within the short span of around a year without the untiring efforts of a large number of persons. We would like to express our gratitude to all those who helped us in this endeavor. We however, deem it our duty to express our gratitude in particular to:

- The contributors for their contributions.
- Mr. Roger Finan of the International Development Research Centre, Delhi for writing a foreword to the volume.
- The Shastri Indo-Canadian Institute for funding the workshop.
- The Planning Unit of the University of Delhi for a publication grant under the head Relevance and Quality of Education and,
- Kaveri Books and, in particular, Mr. Rakesh Goel for being extremely cooperative in bringing out the publication very well and in record time.

– Editors

Foreword

Human activity, increasingly, is resulting in large-scale environmental degradation. It is now obvious, to most people, that our former development activities are neither sustainable nor equitable. Climate change has unquestionably posed a clear and present danger to our global well-being; indeed to the security of our planet. It is an instance of human activity jeopardizing the conditions necessary for the survival of future generations. Environmental sustainability is hence increasingly becoming the accepted goal of most countries of the world. Global governance responses include the UN Framework Convention on Climate Change, the Kyoto Protocol, and the Intergovernmental Panel on Climate Change. Decision-making, that facilitates democratic deliberation and useful action, is challenging even for large "natural resource-rich" and democratic countries like India and Canada. It means fostering procedures of governance that are well informed, inclusive, and responsive.

In India, judicial activism is aiding the enforcement of prevalent legislation to protect the environment and, increased environmental awareness among people is resulting in the adoption of environment-friendly practices and legislation. In Canada, environmental sustainability has been explicitly recognized as one of the priority areas for Canada in the promotion of sustainable development in the new millennium. Sharing experiences would therefore be beneficial to both countries.

The Centre for Canadian Studies of the University of Delhi is to be commended for organizing a three-week workshop on "Sustainable Development: India and Canada" and then publishing this volume, mostly reflecting the presentations debated at the workshop. Indeed, topical multi-disciplinary issues like environment and sustainable development are ones in which research needs to be promoted, knowledge disseminated, and awareness widely increased. This timely publication, "Environment and Sustainable Development: Indo-Canadian Perspectives", addresses the issues without being too technical and hence makes interesting reading for a wide group of readers and users. It is also a truly varied multi-disciplinary volume as its contributors include botanists, economists, engineers, environmental biologists, geographers and geologists. Finally, it combines scholarly abstract theories with practical hands-on experiences–with contributions from university scholars, researchers carrying out applied research, administrators, foresters and representatives of non-government voluntary organizations or apex manufacturers' bodies. The book itself is divided into four parts; it starts with an overview followed by two parts covering various particular sectors – including forestry, and concludes with the fourth part which contains three papers covering conceptual issues.

The book does not claim to be an exhaustive treatise on the subject. Admittedly, all conceptual issues have not been addressed in great depth or detail; nor has the volume covered all the sectors that are relevant or currently topical. For instance, while wind energy is covered there is little discussion on other sources of renewable energy and issues relating to noise or air pollution are simply not addressed. The Canadian component also happens to be somewhat under-represented. The book, simply but masterfully, documents the presentations made at a workshop; to that extent, it is a job well done. Hopefully, the Center for Canadian Studies will maintain its focus on sustainable development leading to further in-depth studies with better coverage and increased Canadian involvement.

As the Regional Director of the International Development Research Centre, in South Asia, I was particularly pleased to have had the opportunity to write the foreword to this book entitled "Environment and Sustainable Development: Indo-Canadian Perspectives". The IDRC is a public corporation created by the Canadian government to help communities in the developing world find solutions to social, economic, and environmental problems through research. At IDRC we set a premium on participatory and multi-disciplinary approaches such as the ones adopted by the Center for Canadian Studies.

Roger Finan
Regional Director
International Development Research Centre
South Asia Regional Office
208 Jor Bagh, New Delhi 110 003

Introduction

It is universally agreed these days that the ecological balance that has sustained itself over years is being seriously upset as a result of increased human activity in blind pursuit of more and more material comforts. Acid rain, global warming, soil erosion, reduction of underground water level, huge reduction of forest cover and the extinction of a number of plant, animal and bird species are mere manifestations of the shape of things to come if there is no stitch in time in this regard. There are, of course, squabbles such as who is more responsible and who should hence pay the lion's share - the developed or the developing countries – for rectifying the currently prevalent state of affairs as regards environmental sustainability. There is, however, increasing awareness and concern, in both developed and developing countries, about the ecological disaster that will befall mankind unless specific measures are taken to ensure environmental sustainability.

Discussions and analysis of these issues cut across disciplines. In most such studies, it is taken for granted that the developed nations of the world became aware of these issues first and then highlighted them to the rest of the world. This is simply not true because there is an equally strong argument that traditional societies were very conscious about the environment and had their effective environmental safeguards as a result of which environmental degradation became a serious problem only after these traditional societies and practices were overthrown by blind commercial exploitation of the environment that the developed nations have been practicing for the past few decades. It is also taken for granted that the well-being of people all over the world will increase if the people of the developing nations are able to adopt the lifestyle of people in the developed nations. The assumption here is that well-being depends merely upon economic growth in terms of per capita net national product, sidelining the stress these days on the quality of life and later developments about subjective indicators of development including indicators of human happiness. A good deal of effort is therefore directed merely to ensure economic growth in the traditional sense without affecting environmental sustainability and to convince entrepreneurs that the pursuit of the environmental goal is not in conflict with profit-maximising calculus. While the importance of such efforts cannot be ignored, it is necessary that more fundamental issues also come up for discussion so that a more holistic view is taken of environmental sustainability taking into account not merely the traditional economic viewpoint, but also the social, political, cultural and other viewpoints.

With all this in mind, the Centre for Canadian Studies, University of Delhi organized a three-week workshop on Sustainable Development between the 23rd of March and the 12th of April 2001. The workshop was on "Sustainable Development: India and Canada" and was funded jointly by the Shastri Indo-Canadian Institute and the Indian Association for Canadian Studies. The Centre could also elicit the co-operation of the International Development Research Centre, the Canadian International Development Agency and the India-Canada Environment Facility. Special efforts were made to ensure that the workshop was truly multi-disciplinary and that a holistic view was taken of sustainability. The multi-disciplinary nature was taken care of by seeing to it that those who were invited to make presentations at the workshop included scholars from disciplines as diverse as Economics, Engineering, Environmental Biology, Forestry, Geography and Geology. A holistic approach, already generated by this multi-disciplinary composition of the scholars invited as speakers, was further strengthened by the participation of senior officials of the Governments of India and Canada dealing with the problem of sustainability and environmental protection and of representatives from application–oriented research organizations like the Tata Energy Research Institute, from apex manufacturers' organizations like the Confederation of Indian Industry and from active non-government organizations engaged in promoting sustainability like Winrock International and the Society for the Promotion of Wastelands Development.

The workshop attracted sixteen participants from different parts of India and went off very well with considerable meaningful interaction between the participants and the twentyfour experts who came to make presentations as well as among the participants themselves. There was therefore a unanimous view at the end of the workshop that a volume consisting of the presentations made at the workshop, revised in the light of the discussions during the workshop, be brought out and hence this volume. The fourteen presentations in the volume are split, for the convenience of the reader, into four parts. Part one gives an overview of the issues involved and consists of three presentations. Part two has four papers all dealing with issues related to forest management. Part three again has four papers all of which deal with specific sectoral aspects of the sustainability issue. The last part is devoted to certain conceptual issues and contains three papers.

Part one giving an overview begins with the inaugural address by Robert Andrigo, the Deputy High Commissioner for Canada in India. In a well-researched address, Andrigo stresses the need for a new approach to environmental management to prevent environmental instability. According to him, the approaches so far have been characterized by mere responses to particular environmental crises as and when they arise without taking a long-term perspective. He feels that people look upon environmental practices as drags on productivity and additions to costs instead of considering them as sources of future competitive advantage. He points out three features of modern development - increasing evidence of the strains of human activity on the eco-sphere, resurgence in public values and action towards environmental protection and the growing recognition in the market place and among business for measures of environmental protection to remain economically competitive. He is of the view that these features make it particularly imperative to bring about a new architecture of environmental management. He also stresses the need to influence the economic and political forces that drive globalisation to act in the service of the environment. The second paper in part one is by Liz Fajber and is entitled Canada and Sustainable Development. It highlights some Canadian perspectives and activities on sustainable development both within Canada and internationally, with special focus on International Development Research Centre's (IDRC) approaches and activities in South Asia. It is pointed out that the four key areas identified in this regard in Canada are pollutants and human health, environmental sustainability, urban ecosystem health and globalisation, which are all of crucial importance also to India. The manner in which Canada is tackling these issues is discussed and two instances in this regard - the appointment in 1995 of a Commissioner for Environment and Sustainable Development responsible for carrying out environmental audits of government activities and the preparation of a Green Report and the initiation in 1994 of a National Round Table on the Environment and the Economy are discussed in some detail. The rest of the paper deals with Canada and international sustainable development and gives the details regarding the IDRC, set up in 1970 by Canada to help developing countries use science and knowledge to find practical and long-term solutions to the social, environmental and economic problems that they face.

It is clearly pointed out how the IDRC attempts to achieve its goal of sustainable development in developing countries using knowledge as the key, research as the means and people as the vehicle. The last paper in part one by D. Mukherjee deals with Environment and Sustainable Development in the Indian Tradition. Mukherjee provides adequate evidence from ancient Indian texts to show that environmental issues were very much kept in mind by people even in ancient India. He quotes a number of instances of the prescriptions of clear do's and don'ts with regard to human environment to maintain ecological balance. The clear recognition of five fundamental elements of environment – land, water, radiation, wind and cosmic space - and the veneration given to forests, trees, plants and mother earth are all amply illustrated by quotations from ancient Indian texts. In view of all this, he is of the opinion that to conserve the environment, we should draw from all religions and cultures. He actually makes a plea for the inclusion of the spiritual dimension in environmental management.

The first paper in part two dealing with forest management is the one by P.C.Tiwari and is entitled Commercial Forestry and its Impact on Natural Environment and Community Sustainability in British Columbia. Tiwari begins his paper by pointing out the fact that forest resources the world over are depleting and degrading and hence stresses the need to have a common definition about what constitutes sustainable forest management. His paper is a study of forestry in the province of British Columbia in the light of the emerging issues in this regard. After giving a detailed overview of forest resources in British Columbia, he discusses in detail the environmental, economic and social impacts of commercial forestry in the province. His inference is that the use of forests mainly for commercial benefits has resulted in the degradation and depletion of critical components of natural environment and has also adversely affected community sustainability. He makes a strong plea for a change in forest management policies with increased public participation and focus on conservation of biodiversity, which according to him is the source of future productivity. The second paper in this section is by Vanita Suneja and gives a brief review of Joint Forest Management(JFM) in India. The paper is split into three parts. Part one gives a brief review of the scenario regarding forestry in India and puts JFM in this context. Part two contains a good account of the principles underlying JFM and also examines in detail the extent to which the practice of JFM has been able to achieve the objects set for the scheme. The findings of the study, brought together in the concluding part, seem to suggest that the concept of JFM is certainly aimed at shifting the people– forest department relation in a desirable direction. The study also points out that JFM has succeeded, among other things, in regenerating forestry. A fear is expressed that the forest department may, in an attempt to regain its fort of control over forestry, devise means like community forestry to jeopardize successfully running JFM schemes. The third paper of this part is a detailed discussion of the National Forestry Action Programme(NFAP) in India by M. Satyanarayana. It begins by giving the international context in which the Tropical Forest Action Plan(TFAP) was launched in 1985 necessitating the formulation of NFAPs for particular nations to translate the global TFAP into the national setting consistent with national priorities and development plans. It then traces out the history of the NFAP in India and goes on to give considerable details in this regard of the NFAP in India. The main components of the programme - protection of existing forest resources, improvement of forest productivity, reduction in total demand placed on forests, strengthening of policy and institutional framework and expansion of forest area - are each taken up for brief discussion. The author however is of the view that in the light of the enormous requirement of resources to successful carry out this programme, unless sufficient resources get generated through international donor agencies, it may not be possible to see it through with the help only of domestic resources. The last paper of this section is a comparison of experiences relating to joint forest management in India and in Canada by

K.R.G.Nair. The comparison is between Dalki in the state of Orissa in India and Temagami in the province of Ontario in Canada. In the introduction, it is pointed out that sustainable development of forests is a complicated goal in view of the large number of stake-holders and often conflicting interests of these groups. The paper then goes on to discuss the details regarding forest development in Dalki and in Temagami respectively. After comparing the two experiences, it is inferred that for sustainable development of forests the importance of non-timber forest produce to meet the subsistence requirements of the forest people should be taken into proper account and that all stake-holders including the original inhabitants should have a say in formulating and implementing policies in this regard. The author also stresses the need to carry out more detailed studies comparing the regional experiences in this regard in both countries to draw more definite and detailed inferences in this regard.

Part three dealing with sectoral aspects has four papers. The first paper by V. Raghuraman is on "Sustainable Development and the Indian Energy Sector". The paper amply demonstrates the need to promote energy - efficiency in India at its present juncture of economic development. It is clearly shown that per capita consumption of primary energy in India is very low and as India develops economically, this level will go up substantially resulting in greater emissions of green house gases. According to the paper, this is all the more so because energy - intensity in India is already very high, there is predominance of coal in energy generation and coal has a very high CO_2 emission coefficient making India the sixth largest carbon dioxide emitter in the world. The paper points out that if all this is considered along with the fact that India might be the world's most populated country by 2025, it is imperative for India to take measures to decouple energy from GDP growth as is being done by many countries of the world. The paper identifies the details in this regard pointing out the sectors and sector-specific policies for India in particular keeping in mind the Kyoto Protocol and on the basis of the results of another detailed study conducted by

Credit Rating Information Services of India Limited. The paper makes particular mention of the fact that the universal adoption of the Kyoto protocol can also help developing countries like India to attract foreign investment to the field of environment. The second paper in this section by Chintan Shah contains an in-depth economic analysis of wind energy development in India and is entitled "Policy and Institutional Issues in Grid Connected Wind Energy Development in India". It traces out the history of development of wind energy in India. It is pointed out that while in the 80s the emphasis was on demonstration projects, the focus was on privatization and indigenisation in early 90s and there was considerable stress on institutional reforms, restructuring and commercialization from 1992 onwards. The paper then goes on to analyse in detail the economic reasons for the sudden fall in investment in this sector in India after the mid-90s after the explosive growth in this regard in the preceding years. The policy inference drawn is that power generation from wind has to become competitive with coal-based electricity in India by providing a stable policy environment, promotion of growth in demand, ensuring attractive buy-back prices and proper institutional facilitation. As regards the supply side, the paper stresses the need to improve capacity, reduce cost and involve developers also in the designing and planning of wind power projects instead of continuing the present practice of solely manufacturer-driven wind power development taking place in India. The third paper of this section is by Prithipalsingh and is entitled "Plants in Delhi's Environment".The paper begins by stressing the role of plants in human life and environment and giving a brief overview of the Geography and Geology of Delhi with particular emphasis on the ridge. It then goes on to enumerate in detail the plants in Delhi covering both the ridge and the riverine tract. A detailed listing is done not only of permanent vegetation, but also ephemeral ones. A description is also given of weeds and cultivated plants of gardens and parks. The fact that 40% of Delhi's plant cover is either introduced or cultivated is clearly brought out and so is the fact that the composition of vegetation in Delhi has undergone change over time. The paper ends with a plea to prevent further degradation of Delhi's environment by maintaining both the quantity and quality of greenery in Delhi. The last paper of this section is by Ganpat S. Roonwal and is entitled "Overview of Human Impacts on the Coastal Ecosystem." Attention is focused initially on the experiences from the coastal zone in Orissa, but lessons from development in this regard from the whole of India are brought into the picture later on. After introducing the topic and specifying the coastal zone, the paper goes on to discuss in detail the human impact, from the environmental point of view, on the coastal zone. The inference drawn is that ineffective planning and management of coastal zones, the absence of environmental impact assessment, inadequate incorporation of environmental issues into feasibility, population pressure as well as increased economic activity are threatening the integrity of coastal ecosystems. The paper welcomes the recent measures taken by the government to protect coastal ecosystems, but suggests that special training be given to government staff regarding general as well as specialized aspects of coastal ecosystem management from the environmental point of view.

Part four dealing with conceptual issues contains three papers. In the paper entitled "Lack of Basic Environmental Infrastructure in Slums and the Ecological Footprint of the Urban Poor," Anjali Bhardwaj has made a qualitative assessment of the "ecological footprint" of the urban poor in developing countries. It is shown that the concept of ecological footprint, developed by Prof. Wackernagel (Director of Indicator's Programme, Redefining Progress, San Francisco), is designed to estimate the impact of human activity on the environment. In the developed world, the ecological footprint takes into account consumption pattern and waste generation. The urban poor in developing countries live in very poor environmental conditions with little or no facilities like sewage, health care, waste disposal etc. The author examines how these factors contribute to the large ecological footprint of this class of society. The paper also discusses different programmes being adopted across the world to improve the living condition of slum dwellers and highlights the importance of NGOs in this context. In the paper entitled "Firm Location in a Spatial Model with Pollution," Yamini Gupt investigates the impact of pollution generated by a duopolist located upstream along a river on a downstream firm and consumers. In the presence of this externality, the firms do not locate in a socially optimal manner. The location decisions of the firms are affected by different parameters including transportation cost and pollution intensity. The study explores different policy options including liability rules, internalization, taxes and zoning that could minimize the pollution cost and total cost to society (defined as the sum of pollution and transportation costs). The results of the simulations indicate that for certain combinations of the parameter values, regulating the locations of the firms through a land use police like zoning may be the appropriate policy option for ensuring sustainable development. In the paper entitled, "Economic Valuation of Wetlands: Problems and Prospects," Amit Love, Shvetank Sharma, Radhey Shyam Sharma and C.R. Babu present a framework for the economic valuation of wetland ecosystems based on a classification of different economic values (direct use, indirect use, option and existence). They emphasize on wetland ecosystems because they are the most productive in the biosphere and are facing increasing threats from developmental activities. The authors highlight the benefits of wetland ecosystems which include fish, fodder, fuelwood and other intangible services like biochemical cycling and nutrient retention etc. Over the years, lack of information about the benefits and economic value, market failure (most goods and services received from these ecosystems are not traded in markets) and the resulting policy failure have led to over - utilization of this resource. The need for economic valuation of this resource gains importance in this context and is essential for devising strategies for sustainable development. The paper also cites examples of some studies in this area and points out some limitations of valuation including its inability to account for the complexities of ecological processes.

Contents

Contributors

R. Andrigo
Deputy High Commissioner for Canada in India

C.R. Babu
Director, Centre for Environmental Management of Degraded Ecosystems, Centre of Excellence, Ministry of Environment and Forests, Government of India and Pro-Vice-Chancellor, University of Delhi

Anjali Bhardwaj,
Senior Programme Officer, Winrock International India

Liz Fajber,
Regional Programme Officer, International Development Research Center- South Asian Regional Office

Amit Love,
Centre for Environmental Management of Degraded Ecosystems, Centre of Excellence, Ministry of Environment and Forests, Government of India

D. Mukherjee,
Sparta Institute of Social Studies. NOIDA

Prithipalsingh,
Department of Botany, Kirori Mal College, University of Delhi, Delhi

V. Raghuraman
Senior Adviser-Energy, Confederation of Indian Industry, New Delhi

M. Satyanarayana,
Deputy Inspector General of Forests, Ministry of Environment and Forests, Government of India

Chintan Shah,
Tata Energy Research Institute, New Delhi

Radhey Shyam Sharma
Centre for Environmental Management of Degraded Ecosystems, Centre of Excellence, Ministry of Environment and Forests, Government of India

Shvetank Sharma
Centre for Environmental Management of Degraded Ecosystems, Centre of Excellence, Ministry of Environment and Forests, Government of India

Vanita Suneja,
Programme Officer, Society for Promotion of Wastelands Development

P.C. Tiwari,
Department of Geography, Kumaon University, Uttaranchal

❑❑❑

PART-I

An Overview

Inaugural Address

1

R. Andrigo

I am delighted to be here today in this distinguished University; and I am particularly pleased and honoured to be addressing a group of scholars who share a common goal of expanding Indo-Canadian ties via the vehicle of the study of Canada in India.

The bedrock of any relationship between countries is its people-to-people dimension; and, in this regard, the academic relations component is perhaps pre-eminent because it underpins the mutual understanding between and among the intellectual opinion-makers and leaders, both of today and tomorrow, that increasingly is critical in an ever more interdependent and complex world.

I have been asked today to speak on the topic of Sustainable Development, a task that I join with decided humility given the complexities of the subject and the intimidating fact of an expert audience far better versed than I in the intricacies of the subject. So, to dispel any personal conceits on this score, I shall, at the outset, register the general caveat framed by the wise man who said that none of us is exempt from talking nonsense, the misfortune is to do so solemnly, I shall, accordingly, be suitably irreverent.

As the millennial clock turned over this January, we heard vastly different predictions from different commentators. On one side, assurances that we are in the middle of a "long boom" that will bring unparalleled economic growth to all parts of the world, driven by information technology, biotechnology, nano-technology, and other breakthroughs.

On the other, there were warnings that our economies are already straining the limits of the earth's carrying capacity, and that thirty more years of unchecked growth could push us past the breaking point. You have to ask: Where are we headed?

Towards global peace and prosperity, or towards increasing ecological tensions, with climate change leading to further flooding, dustbowls and world food shortages? Perhaps the answer is that both futures are possible, but environmental instability and its consequences will be real if the genius of our technological and e-commerce economy is not turned to solving our environmental challenges with as much diligence as it pursues microchip miniaturization or biotech breakthroughs

No one will dispute that we all would wish for any child born today – whether in Canada or India – to not only grow up to be well-educated, to find ready employment and enjoy a high standard of living, but also to be able to breathe clean air, to swim in clean water, and to enjoy the changing of the seasons and the vast diversity of the earth's plants and creatures.

For this goal to become a reality, we need to pursue not merely economic growth, but more sustainable, more efficient growth. We need to redesign the way we produce wealth, and the way we supply goods and services. We will need clean renewable energy, efficient, clean transportation, zero waste, benign emissions, sustainable fisheries, forestry, agriculture, and livable cities. Achieving this vision calls for new ways of thinking about our environmental responsibilities, whether as individual consumers, companies, communities or governments. This suggests that the old style of environmental management – responding to immediate problems and crises and ignoring longer term costs – must give way to a new architecture of environmental management.

Any such new architecture must consider environmental prudence today to be a firm foundation for building future economic growth, and will conceive of the environment and the economy not as competing, or even complementary, priorities, but as part of an integrated whole. As the social critic Jane Jacobs reminds us in her book, **The Nature of Economies**, the human economy is part of our natural ecology, and economic growth is governed by the same principles and limits that apply to biological growth in nature. A new architecture of environmental management must seek to harness and channel economic forces into sustainable growth, rather than reacting to damage already done. It will need to treat environmental sustainability as a key competitive advantage for the future, not as a drag on productivity. In effect, environmental practices must come to be seen as profit centers not as costs.

The new architecture will set environmental goals for our entire economy and society, and will make governments and businesses accountable for meeting them. I would submit that the need for this new architecture derives from the existence of three trends or developments:

- First, is the increasing evidence of the strains that human activity is placing on the ecosphere;
- Second, is a resurgence in public values and action toward environmental protection; and,
- Third, is a growing recognition within the marketplace, and among business, of the need for environmental change in order to remain economically competitive.

Global Stress of Human Economic Activity

The first trend is the growing – and increasingly obvious – strain that human activity is placing on our global ecosphere. There have been important environmental achievements over the past three decades. But despite these achievements, inefficient human activity and economic growth are continuing to outstrip our successes. The global economy continues to expand rapidly – by an estimated $1 trillion per year and the world's human population is expected to grow to almost 9 billion in the next fifty years.

At the same time, it should come as no surprise that the carrying capacity of the Earth's ecosystems to support human activity has finite limits. If we look at the patterns of human production and consumption and the effects they have had on the planet, we find that, over the past twenty years, the economies of the OECD countries alone have grown by 40%. That's to the good. But at the same time, we have increased our production of waste by an identical 40%. Obviously, we have not yet turned enough of our attention to efficiencies.

Indeed, the U.S. National Academy of Engineering estimates that 93 percent of the materials which go into the production of consumer goods end up as waste before the goods are even sold.

All of this consumption takes a toll on the planet. Every one of us has an "ecological footprint" – the amount of land and water necessary to support our lifestyle. For instance, it takes 7.7 hectares of land to support the lifestyle of the average Canadian. That 7.7 hectare/person footprint is much larger than that of many European countries. For example, each of Germany and the Netherlands have a footprint of 5.3 hectares/person, whereas France has one of 4.2 hectares. All these, are several time the 2.1 hectares that would be available per capita if all of the world's resources were divided equally.

Perhaps nowhere is the impact of human activity on the ecosphere more evident than in the growing threat of global climate change. The trends in global temperature are unmistakable. The 1990s saw the warmest surface temperatures since accurate measurement began around 1860, and climatologists estimate that they are warmer than at any time in the past 1200 years.

The effects of this human-induced temperature increase threaten the entire global ecosystem. Polar ice-caps and glaciers already are rapidly melting, thus increasing global sea levels. All of these factors contribute to climate instability, and to major and costly repercussions on human activity – as India knows only too well. So there can be little doubt that human activity has had a profound effect on the global ecosphere, and that we are stretching the earth's carrying capacity.

The Resurgence of Public Environmental Values

As a result, we are seeing a resurgence in public expressions of environmental values, and a shift in the values of citizens towards an environmental ethic – and, increasingly, towards action. It is not complicated. People around the world want to live in a clean, healthy environment. To cite the Canadian example, Canadians are alarmed by the environmental degradation they have seen in their communities. They now know that air and water pollution are linked to health problems, and when one in four school absences in determined to be caused by childhood asthma, they worry; when air pollution contributes to the death of 5,000 people per year, and hospitalizes many more, they worry. And when almost 100 municipalities have to call for temporary "boil water" days, they worry.And while the situation in Canada is not as dramatic as in many other places in the world where clean water is a rare commodity, these experiences are leading Canadians to a new environmental ethic, as they are in many other countries.

In all this, the generational factor is emerging as a critical element in the equation. As the generation that must deal with the consequences of the environmental debt, it is not surprising that young people have developed a certain urgency for change in our environmental approaches.

They are not content simply to wait for the conventional political process to make slow progress on these issues. Thanks to communications technology, a new kind of e-democracy is emerging, driven by the young, that public decision makers will be unable to ignore. We saw with the protest over the WTO in Seattle, prepared in advance by months of Internet organizing, especially among younger people, the consequences of ignoring public environmental and social concerns.

This emergence of environmental and social non-governmental organizations as players in environmental and economic policy, thus creates a new policy-making dynamic. This resurgence of environmental values – with an emphasis on action – cannot be ignored.

Time to Reconcile Economic and Environmental Interests

These first two trends are creating a new context for business and government alike. And this comprises the third trend – namely, a growing environmental awareness within the marketplace, and a recognition that good environmental practices provide not only good will, but also host competitive advantage.

Leading companies are finding profit centers in best environmental practices. The recent Dow Jones Sustainability Index is finding that those companies with strong environmental practices also are among the most profitable and attractive to investors. Unlike their predecessors, the new generation of young entrepreneurs, MBAs and dotcom workers of Generation X believe strongly in corporate environmental responsibility. They want to help build companies that will support, rather than destroy, our natural environment. These young people see opportunities, not problems, in the growing global environmental marketplace. Concurrently, consumers increasingly are demanding that the products they buy are sustainably produced.

Companies accordingly are responding to market pressures that are causing them to make environmental practices a top priority. As many of you know, a number of companies are adopting a product lifecycle management approach to manufacturing, that requires consideration of the costs and impacts of products at every stage from initial resource extraction to the final consumer. As the shift towards a more environmentally responsive economy unfolds, the most far-sighted companies have decided that, given the underlying pressures for more sustainable practices, long term corporate survival hinges on fundamentally transforming the nature of their businesses. For example, oil companies gradually are repositioning themselves as sustainable energy companies, setting ambitious goals for greenhouse gas reductions, and investing in alternative energy like solar energy cells and photovoltaics; and automobile companies are racing to market hybrid electric vehicles.

We cannot predict exactly how businesses will restructure themselves to respond to environmental imperatives. But what is entirely predictable is that those companies – and those countries – that make the first breakthroughs towards greater sustainability and more efficient technologies will gain major competitive advantages in the twenty-first century.

These, then, are the challenges that public policy must respond to – increasing stress on our global ecosystems, increasing pubic concern and activism on environmental issues, and a rapidly changing marketplace where meeting environmental goals is moving from a costly irritant to a competitive necessity.

Before closing, I should like to touch briefly on globalization. As we saw in Seattle, there exist concerns among our citizenry not only that there is must unfinished environmental business to transact, but that the progress that has been achieved is potentially threatened by globalization.

Notwithstanding the practical impossibility of turning back the clock to the days of closed borders and insular economies, it is questionable, at best, to posit that reversal of globalization would automatically improve the environment. The real, and more productive task, is to influence the economic and political forces that drive globalization so that they act in the service of the environment. The need is to focus inventive minds on reducing energy use and resource consumption, to tackle the problem of clean transportation, more liveable cities and sustainable rural regions.

This perhaps suggests the need for a new architecture of environmental management. One that necessarily will involve a more imaginative set of tools than the traditional legislative, and regulatory command and control mechanisms that have become the reflexive norm. New ways need to be found to co-operate, and to stimulate socially and environmentally acceptable behavior. Undoubtedly, the market might be expected to play a constructive role in this mission.

I expect that your discussions in the course of this workshop will range over these many challenges, and that you will bring your collective creativities to bear on the problem. For these inquiries and speculations that you will engage, I wish you a fruitful and productive dialogue.

Canada and Sustainable Development

2

Liz Fajber

Introduction

As the new millennium approaches, Canada and the rest of the world face immense challenges and opportunities for sustainable development. These complex problems require complex solutions that reconcile economic, environmental and social concerns at local, regional, national and global levels. This paper highlights some Canadian perspectives and activities on sustainable development, both within Canada and internationally. In regards to the latter, it focuses primarily on International Development Research Centre's (IDRC) approaches and activities in South Asia.

> "The purpose of Canadian international assistance is to support sustainable development in developing nations, in order to reduce poverty and contribute to a more secure, equitable and prosperous world"
>
> *Canada in the World*, DFAIT

As a significant component to this approach, Canada has dedicated itself to addressing the challenges outlined by the Brundtland Commission on Sustainable Development and towards supporting equitable and sustainable growth in developing nations, as well as in Canada.

Sustainable development is development that meets the basic needs of the present population without diminishing the ability of future generations to meet their own. While environmental sustainability is an essential component of overall global sustainable development, Canadian programs emphasize the importance of integrating economic, political, social and cultural sustainability with environmental programs. No one area operates independently of the others: all factors are inextricably linked. Poverty, gender equality, human security, ecological integrity, knowledge systems, human rights and economy must all be considered in sustainable development programming.

Environmental sustainability, from a Canadian perspective includes maintaining both ecosystem integrity and biological diversity. Developing community capacity to sustainably use and manage their natural resources is essential.

Economic sustainability is needed to promote efficient and equitable economic development with an aim to increasing the wellbeing of the poor without negative consequences to the environment. A focus must be placed on poverty alleviation to reduce demand on natural resources, which is intimately linked to environmental sustainability. Sound economic management is seen as the key to raising the developmental status of poor countries, especially in light of present day globalization.

Notably, **political sustainability** is also critical as it fosters the political will and capacities of societies to both respect the rights of women and men, and to govern effectively in a democratic manner. How societies structure and govern themselves, make decisions and distribute power affects the area's economic, social, cultural and environmental development.

And lastly, **social and cultural sustainability** is promoted through social well-being, gender equity, and a recognition of cultural values and context. Improved income distribution and investment in the social sector contribute to social well-being. These must be done in an equitable manner which aim for a fair distribution of costs and benefits, and which meet peoples' basic needs and rights. Development must include careful assessment and analysis of cultural environments and knowledge systems. This requires understanding how local communities generate and use knowledge. The goal is to help find innovative, locally appropriate means of sustainable development.

Sustainable Development in Canada

In turning our attention to sustainable development issues in Canada, I would like to outline four key areas which have been highlighted in a recent discussion paper entitled *"Sustainable Development Priorities for the New Millenium"* put together by the National Round Table on the Environment and the Economy. These four areas are: pollutants and human health, environmental sustainability, urban ecosystem health, and globalization. It is worth noting that these core areas are similar to issues facing India, although of course in a different context and scale.

Pollutants and Human Health

Human health problems have risen dramatically in Canada, with linkages to environmental pollutants becoming an increasing concern. The effects of long term exposure to pollutants are still unknown, and there is concern that many pollutants may cause subtle but widespread damage to human health. Notably, the unborn, young and elderly are particularly affected as their immune and neurological systems are especially vulnerable, making them more susceptible to learning disabilities, diminished intellectual capacity and diseases in general. Given the lack of knowledge about the combined effects of pollutants on health, significant resources need to be devoted to monitoring and researching impacts of pollutants on human health.

Environmental Sustainability

Canada depends on its natural resources for resource-based industry, tourism, and ecological sustainability. However, pressure on Canadian natural resources has grown at an unprecedented rate. Natural wildlife habitat, is increasingly fragmented by industrial development, roads, agriculture, and urban development. Over 340 species are at risk of extinction in Canada, and that number is growing. New integrated systems of land management are needed in ways that balance the need for resources, livelihoods of inhabitants, and the integrity of ecosystems. This must include participation from the range of stakeholders involved: governments, private landowners, resource industries, non-government organizations, rural communities, and Aboriginal peoples.

Urban Ecosystem Health

Canada is a highly urbanized country. Most people live, work and develop in urban centers. However, rapid urbanization combined with poor planning has led to urban sprawl, inadequate infrastructure, poor air quality, contaminated sites, and loss of buildings with heritage or historical value. The adverse effects tend to fall disproportionately upon disadvantaged and marginalized groups including the poor. Notably, increasing privatization of public services such as water control and quality has led to some recent problems of inadequate monitoring resulting in sickness and some deaths, as exemplified in the town of Walkerton, Ontario.

The public sector needs to pay adequate attention to these issues, and collaborate with the private sector and community activists to implement urban planning to meet community needs and health.

Globalization

Increasing global trade linkages of not only resources, but also knowledge and technology, are reorienting the make-up of many national economies, including Canada. Canada, whose economy has traditionally been resource-intensive, must now diversify to one of services, information and technologies, in order to be competitive. Industries must address global environmental concerns and minimize waste and ensure sustainability of resources. In order to achieve these appropriate market systems, fiscal policies will need to be developed and implemented.

What is Canada doing to respond?

Canada is aiming to respond to these challenges through:

- an integrated approach recognizing environmental, economic and social components of development
- increasing investments in scientific research and monitoring capacity in order to manage- to understand, track, and predict- environmental change.
- involving all sectors in dialogue and action: government, industry, academics, communities, Aboriginal peoples, local NGOs
- directing our actions to implement change – through policy and its implementation at local, national and international levels.

At a parliamentary level, Canada has made several commitments and actions to sustainable development. One such commitment is the 1995 Amendment to the Auditor-General's Act which called for the establishment of a **Commissioner of Environment and Sustainable Development**. Every government department must table a "Sustainable Development Strategy" that the commissioner evaluates. The commissioner, who is currently Johanne Gelinas, is also responsible for conducting environmental audits of departments and submitting a "Green Report" to the Parliament on government activities.

Another example of a national initiative is the **National Round Table on the Environment and the Economy**

(NRTEE). Legislated by Parliament in 1994, NRTEE explains and promotes sustainable development. It is an independent advisory body that provides decision-makers, opinion leaders and the Canadian public with advice and recommendations concerning sustainable development. Members, appointed by the Canadian prime minister, represent a wide range of regions and sectors, including business, labour, academia, environmental organizations and First Nations.

In collaboration with these stakeholders, the NRTEE identifies key issues with both environmental and economic implications and supports further research and informed discussion, with an aim to come up with solutions which may meet the needs of the often conflicting views of different stakeholders, while balancing economic prosperity with environmental sustainability.

As such, the NRTEE has adopted a round table format bringing all the stakeholders to the table that aims to:

- analyze environmental and economic facts and trends;
- assimilate research and consultation to clarify the debate;
- pinpoint the consequences of action and inaction, and making recommendations.

Examples of current program topics include:

- Environment and Sustainable Development Indicators Initiative
- Eco-efficiency
- Economic Instruments
  - Ecological Fiscal Reform
  - Green Budget Reform
- Sustainable Development Issues for the New Millennium
- Health, Environment and the Economy

- Aboriginal Communities and Non-renewable Resources Development

As part of the program on Aboriginal Communities and Non-Renewable Resources Development, the NRTEE has established a taskforce to investigate the Mackenzie Valley region in the Northwest Territories. This area is rich in oil and gas, diamonds and other minerals. It is also an area inhabited primarily by Aboriginal communities and disputed land claims and rights and access to resources. This task force is conducting research on the opportunities related to these resources, legal and regulatory frameworks, impacts and benefit agreements in addition to environmental and social impacts of development in this sector. The aim is to bring these diverse groups together to discuss some of the opportunities and consequences of development to identify strategies which will support economically viable, self-sufficient Aboriginal communities without compromising the ecological integrity of the environment, or retention of social structures and cultures.

Canada and International Sustainable Development

Turning now to the international context, it is worth noting that Canadian sustainable development assistance is an integral part of our foreign policy. As set by Canada's International Development Agency (CIDA)'s Sustainable Development Strategy 2001-2003, Overseas Development Assistance seeks to achieve three broad objectives:

1) Through investment in prosperity and employment, Canada is contributing to social and economic growth. In the long run, this develops a stronger global economy and helps connect economies and enhance trade relations.

2) By fighting against human security threats such as population growth, disease, environmental degradation, human rights abuses and the widening gap between the world's rich and poor, Canada aims to contribute to long-term global security; and

3) Canada is committed to social justice, democratic governance and participatory government.

Canada has also committed to a number of international environmental agreements including the Convention on Biological Diversity, the Framework Convention on Climate Change and Kyoto Protocol, the RAMSAR convention, the Convention on International Trade of Endangered Species and others.

One component of Canada's program of development assistance is the **International Development Research Centre (IDRC):** IDRC is a public corporation created by the Parliament of Canada in 1970 to help developing countries use science and knowledge to find practical, long-term solutions to the social, environmental, and economic problems they face.

Support is directed toward developing indigenous research capacity to sustain policies and technologies developing countries need to build healthier, more equitable, and more prosperous societies.

Our mission statement highlights that:

- **Knowledge is the key**. Sustainable improvements in human well-being depend on knowledge, its production, distribution, ownership, and wise application.
- **Research is the means**. Research done in and by a country is vitally important for the production of knowledge needed for its development.
- **People are the vehicle**. Development takes place when men, women and their communities develop the ability to identify and solve their own problems.
- **Sustainable and equitable development is the goal**. IDRC is pledged to the generation and use of knowledge in ways that alleviate poverty and improve people's lives.

IDRC Approach

IDRC aims to develop appropriate sustainable development programs and projects dependent on local and national needs and priorities. Our programs are multidisciplinary and holitic in nature and address a problem from an issues-oriented, rather than disciplinary approach. We promote programs which integrate the participation and interests of all stakeholders, and to maximize the impact, we emphasize the need for collaboration, networking and exchange of information, experience and process. The research we support is directed towards informing the policy arena (local, national and international) so that decision-makers may make informed decisions based on sound research and analysis

IDRC Program Areas

There exists a daunting inventory of global problems: conflict, poverty, environmental devastation and the digital divide between the North and South. Development organisations have to choose which problems to tackle and how to make programming respond to the varying needs of the different regions in which it works. Recognising that the components of complex issues cannot be isolated into single disciplines, IDRC has taken a multidisciplinary approach to tackling development problems through three broad Program Areas:

- Social and Economic Equity
- Environment and Natural Resource Management
- Information and Communication Technologies

Social and Economic Equity

Economic stabilization in the face of adjustment programs requires policies that compensate the poor and take into account environmental sustainability- both losers in the process of economic globalization. Leaders and decision-makers can formulate policies designed to reduce poverty and economic vulnerability, but there need to be mechanisms to ensure their effective implementation.

IDRC is working in four areas to address these issues:

- Support for governance to ensure that public institutions are more representative and accountable.
- Delivering public services – health, education, social security – in ways that are more effective, equitable and financially sustainable.
- Helping developing countries deal with the effects of some of the instruments of globalisation, notably the rules and codes of the World Trade Organization.
- Supporting people, particularly women and youth, in their struggle to find secure jobs and earn an income.

Environment and Natural Resource Management

Degradation of natural resources (air, water, forests, land) and the depletion of species are increasing at an alarming rate. A large proportion of the population does not have access to safe drinking water, ground water depletion is widespread, and the contamination of groundwater with arsenic, fluoride, and other toxins has affected the health of millions of people. There is a need to ensure that marginalized communities have access to the resources for their daily life and livelihood needs.

The complexity of environment and natural resource management demands research to help achieve the following:

- Ensuring secure sources of food and water for the poor by focusing on institutional development, production technology, local resource management, and appropriate policy choices.
- Improving human health and well-being by managing ecosystems better.
- Protecting local management and control of biodiversity in the light of global initiatives and policies governing genetic resources.

One example of a project addressing these issues in South Asia is on "**Local Strategies for Water Supply and**

Conservation Management". Many traditional approaches to water management, focus on quick-fix, large-scale solutions such as mega- dams and vast irrigation systems and often exclude most of the population from participating as stakeholders in the process. This project takes an alternative approach to water management by supporting innovative local solutions to water scarcity and pollution and by considering all stakeholders.

The project is using a Water Evaluation and Planning modeling system called WEAP, to enable systematic quantitative analysis of water demand and supply management options. WEAP generates scenarios for different levels of water supply (such as rainfall, water table levels, climate, water harvesting) and demand (such as sprinkler use, irrigation, crop demand, human consumption etc.) and estimates how they will affect the future status of water. The research allows stakeholders to look 10 years down the road and see a picture of the impact of current water management practices.

The modeling system enables researchers to evaluate how communities can better manage their water resources to ensure sustainable supply and equitable supply distribution. It also provides a basis for building stakeholder consensus, by identifying potential solutions and creating a common framework for understanding and discussion. The project, a collaborative effort between five research institutes in India and Nepal and the US, also has a significant networking component on sharing experience, methodologies and expertise.

Information and Communication Technologies (ICTs) Issues:

As the ICT world rapidly changes, the divide between the information rich and information poor is expanding. To help bridge this gap, IDRC is exploring how local groups and the research and development community can use ICTs to solve development problems that also promote accessibility and equity.

Research efforts concentrate on the following:

- Equitable and sustainable access to information and to the use of ICTs so that all of society benefits; and
- Developments in the information economy. This includes the concerns of communities and businesses, e-commerce, and the local effects of global trade rules.

One example of the PAN Asia program is a telecenter project with the M.S. Swaminathan Research Foundation in South India. The project has successfully developed five village telecentres around Pondicherry. Each centre provides villages with access to relevant internet and database information from health and education to public welfare schemes and government charters to agricultural practices and weather reports. As a result, farmers have been able to share critical information on pest management of sugarcane, get better prices for their produce and access to better quality seeds; women from families with no assets have managed to get health insurance; and fishermen's lives are being saved by warning of wave conditions garnered from satellite images. Each telecentre is run by trained, local volunteers, half of whom are women.

Conclusion

These are just a few examples of IDRC supported activities in South Asia. However, the challenges of sustainable development are certainly a global concern. Canada recognizes the need to address these issues both at national and international levels. IDRC is but one component of Canada's program towards tackling the complexity and multi-level nature of these issues. In South Asia, as well as other regions in the world, IDRC is committed to supporting researchers, activists and policy-makers to address the complex challenges of sustainable development.

Environment and Sustainable Development in the Indian Tradition

3

D. Mukherjee

Introduction

It is only during the last few decades that the people, in general, have been getting more and more concerned about the urgent need for protecting the delicate ecological balance. Many of the countries have now been enacting specific environmental laws with a view of effecting improvement of the fast deteriorating environment. But, as a matter of fact, the need to maintain the human environment in a healthy state cannot be a new concern of the modern society, for even in the earlier times, environmental issues were indeed kept in mind, albeit indirectly, while interacting with nature. Ancient Indian texts show that the people were concerned about the vulnerability of the environment and hence they prescribed various do's and don'ts with regard to human environment, so that the ecological balance could be maintained. Even while framing the normal civil codes of conduct and laws, environmental issues were not overlooked. Adequate provisions were made in the ancient Indian laws, offering necessary legal protection for betterment of the ecology and human environment.

General concern for natural ecology was expressed in the ancient Indian thoughts, encompassing all the five traditional elements of natural environment, namely: land (ksiti), water (ap), radiation or energy (tejas), wind (marut) and cosmic space (vyoman), and their relation with human activities. No specific ancient work on the science of ecology, however, has come to light, perhaps because there was no historical necessity to have such works at that time. But many of the instructions recorded in the holy scriptures and traditional texts on ethics and law indicate the existence of positive approaches.

Natural Resource Management in Ancient India

Hymn RigVeda X: 146 is addressed to the lady of the Forest, Aranyani, "she who tills not yet has stores of food" a sentence that clearly expresses the concept of sacred forest; she becomes fearful and destructive towards those who trespass her law. Aranyani is the invisible personification of the forest. "She seems to vanish from sight" as one advances in the forest; she is the spirit, the concept, the form or essence, the energy, the virtual reality and intellectual formulation of the forest. She is feminine, because as a mother, she gives her all asking only for devotion, care and love in return. She is unforgiving towards those who harm her and through her, harm her obedient children. She is the idea of the unending exchange of matter and energy that goes on in the forest and in the clearings where the cattle graze. She rejoices with the sounds of life in herself, she has stores of food which she gives off freely to the deserving ones, according to the law". There can hardly be a better rendering of the concept of the forest ecosystem in poetical yet correct terms.

The tree is the most prominent element of the forest, hence it becomes the materialized symbol of the bounties offered by the forest. In India, people worshipped the tree, some of them in a particular manner, the pipul (Ficus religiosa) being the most important among them, as a symbol of life and regeneration. Both Kalpavriksha and Kamadhenu are symbols of nature's generosity, if, and only if nature is revered, respected, obeyed and used according to its own rules and laws.

The symbiotic relationship between earth and living beings has been enuniciated in Brahad aranyaka-Upnishad (2/5/1), like:

> "This earth (iyam prithivi) is helpful to all living beings (sarvesam bhutanam madhu); all living being are of helpful effect (srvani bhutani madhu) to the earth (asyai prithivyai)"
>
> (Barhad-aranyaka-Upanisad 2/5/1)

The above passage clearly implies that while the mother earth, no doubt, produces and sustains the entire biosphere, the mankind and other members of the biosphere also, in their turn, must be shaping and sustaining the earth adequately on sound principles of economy. A Vedic prayer expressing almost similar sentiments, runs as follows:

> "May the plants and crops, the sun and the stars and the waters be as sweet as honey (madhumatir osadhir dyava apah). Let the firmament be sweet to us (madhuman-no bhavanta antariksam). To us let the farmers be sweet (ksetrasya patir madhuman no astu) and may we follow the footsteps of these farmers, unhindered (arisyanto any enam carema)"
>
> (Rig-Veda Samhita 4/57/3)

The punishment meted out to the environmental offenders in ancient India used to vary according to the gravity of the offence committed, and in this regard, the prescription of Manu (circa 2300 BC) in respect of offence against the plant kingdom, for example, is –

> "The violence against trees, etc., would attract appropriate punishment in different degrees (tatha tatha damah karyo

> himsayam iti dharana), depending upon the usefulness or importance of different part of the plant (vanaspatinam sarvesam upabhogo yatha yatha)".
>
> (Manu-smriti 8/285)

All the punishments prescribed in our scriptures and ancient law books for offences committed against bio-diversity and against the living plants in particular may appear, in the context of the present-day world, to be rather naïve and somewhat outlandish. But these scriptural injunctions and provisions of law must have had sufficient moral and legal force to act as deterrents to the commitment of environmental offences at that time (Das Gupta, 1995). Had it been not so, this vast sub-continent of our world would have been completely stripped of all trees centuries ago. Unfortunately, despite much stricter laws of modern times, our forest canopy is fast vanishing at an alarming rate and our wildlife is getting extinct faster and faster.

Hinduism teaches renunciation of worldly goods and preaches against materialism and consumerism. Such teachings could act as a great source of strength for Hindu societies in their struggle to achieve sustainable development. Until very recently, the role of our cultural and spiritual heritages in environmental protection and sustainable development was ignored by international bodies, national governments, policy planners, and even environmentalists. Many fear that bringing religion into the environmental movement will threaten objectivity, scientific investigation, professionalism, or democratic values. But none of these need to be displaced in order to include the spiritual dimension in environmental protection. That dimension, if introduced in the process of environmental policy planning, administration, education, and law, could help create a self-consciously moral society which would put conservation and respect for God's creation first, and relegate individualism, materialism, and our modern desire to dominate nature to a secondary place.

First, religion defends the individual's existence against the depersonalizing effects of the techno-industrial process. Second, it forces the individual to recognize human fallibility and to combine realism with idealism. Third, while technology gives the individual the physical power to create or to destroy the world, religion gives the moral strength to grow by nurturing restraints, humility, and liberation from self-centeredness. Religion can be a powerful source for environmental conservation and protection. Thus, we need a strategy for conservation that does not ignore the powerful influence of religions, but instead draws from all religious foundations and cultures.

Plants are frequently invoked as divinities, chiefly along with waters, rivers, mountains, heaven and earth. One entire hymn (x: 97) of the Rigveda is, however, devoted to the praise of plants or osadhi mainly with regard to their healing powers. Later, Vedic texts mention offerings made to plants and the praise of large trees.

The worship of trees in India is in no way surprising. It is the trees and plants that provide food, fuel, fodder and medicine to human beings. Primitive man hunted his food and his prey was mainly animals. But it was the trees and plants that proved to be reliable sources of food. Worship of trees continues even today during the months of May-June. The Aswattha (Ficus religiosa) trees are worshipped because it was under one such tree that Buddha received enlightenment.

Manu Samhita – provides the code of both religious and civil laws. The text has 2,694 verses in 12 chapters. The text contains instructions for conservation of plants and animals. The instructions on conservation of plants and animals are scattered in verses of different chapters. According to Manu Samhita (1.25, 39-45) Brahma, the God of creation has created all the plants and animals with specific characteristics and functions, and none should disturb these creatures.

The text (X.89) mentions that the forest-dwelling animals and birds are not articles for sale. Before enunciating this general instruction, the text states (III.162) that, one who coerces the elephant, cow, horse or camel or maintains falcon for sport or for sale to earn a living, should not be invited to any socio-religious festival. If one cannot make profit by catching wild animals and birds, then why one should face the hazards of trapping them! Thus, it may be said that the above instructions go a long way in saving these creatures from poaching. For saving the plants and their parts from injury/destruction, Manu Samhita prescribes various punishment for the offenders. The fear of punishment(s) acts as a significant deterrent, and greedy people dither to cause harm to the plants. The Manu Samhita states that protecting the animals is the duty of the king. According to this text (VIII. 306), the king who protects animals and punishes the killers earns merits. The text (V.37) categorically prohibits the unwanted slaughter of animals (na tveba tu vrthahantum pasumicchet kadacana). Manu, so severely condemns the unnecessary slaughter of animals that he says (V.38) that the sin of such an act haunts the sinner in birth after birth.

Chapter XVII of Arthashastra, titled "The Superintendent of Forest Produce" points out : "The Superintendent of Forest Produce shall collect timber and other products of forests by employing those who guard productive forests. He shall not only start productive works in forests but also fix adequate fines and compensations to be levied from those who cause any damage to productive forests". Kautilya's Arthasastra prescribed various punishments for destroying trees and plants.

For cutting off the tender sprouts of fruit trees or shady trees in the parks near a city, a fine of six panas shall be imposed; for cutting off the minor branches of the same trees, twelve panas, and for cutting off the big branches, twenty-four panas shall be levied. Cutting off the trunks of the same, shall be punished with the first amercemen; and felling shall be punished with the middlemost amercement" (Kautilya's Arthasastra 2: 19:197)

"The destruction of forest is most dangerous for nations and human beings. Vanaspati has direct relationship with the well-being of the society. Due to the pollution of the natural environment and the destruction of vanaspati, many diseases crop up to ruin the nation. Only then, vanaspati with medicinal qualities may enhance the nature and cure the diseases of human beings". (Charak Samhita 3/11)

Land which cannot be used for agriculture is to be used either for pastures or forests (2.2 1ff). There are two types of forest produce draryavana and the hastivana or the sanctuary for elephants. The latter has little economic value, as the elephants are mainly used in wars (2.2. 13-14) The principal produce of the dravyavana would appear to be timber and wood of all kinds as well as base metals like iron, copper, lead etc. (2.17.4 ff). There can be no doubt that both kinds of forests belong to the state. It is laid down that a separate forest should be planted for each different type of produce (2.2.5). In fact, the Chapter (2.2) creates the impression that entirely new forests are to be planted when a new state is carved out of unoccupied territory. Quite a substantial income may be supposed to come to the state from its forest wealth. There is a special store house in the capital for forest product (2.5.1,5). It seems that some of the raw material produced in the forest is to be turned into finished articles in factories established for the purpose.

Dattatreya is the deity with three heads representing Hindu trinity. He received education and wisdom from twentyfour elements of nature and creation. He took upon himself to protect and conserve the environment. He is the patron saint and presiding deity of the environment.

Conclusion

Traditional societies, deal with bio-diversity and sustainable development in a variety of ways. The manner in which the tribals manipulate crop and associated bio-diversity at species and sub-species levels under varied Jhum cycles of shifting agriculture, transformation of Jhum to sedentary system, and to home gardens – give a clue about their responce to uncertainties in the environment that they have had to cope up with. Similarly, the way traditional societies perceive species within natural ecosystem types at the landscape levels, provide important clues for bio-diversity conservation/management at ecosystem and landscape levels. All these have implications for future response mechanism that need to be integrated into managing ecosystems under threat from 'global change'.

References

Buhler, George (1964), *The Laws of Manu*, Delhi: Motilal Benarsidass.

Dasgupta, S.P. (1995), Environment Laws in Ancient Indian in *Man and Environment*: Calcutta.

Keith, A.B. (1987) *RigVeda*, Delhi: Motilal Banarsidass.

Mukhopadhyay, Durgadas (1993) *Culture, Performance Communication*, Delhi: B.R. Publishing.

Shamashastry (1967), *Kautilya's Arthashastra*, Mysore.

Swami Gambhirananda (1984), *The Eight Upanishads*, Calcutta: Ramakrishna Mission.

Vidyashankar, Jayadev (1984) *Charak Samhita*, Delhi: Motilal Banarasidass.

PART-II

Forest Management

Commercial Forestry and its Impact on Natural Environment and Community Sustainability in British Columbia

4

P.C. Tiwari

Introduction

Forests are a dominant feature and most valuable natural resource on the earth's landscape. We depend on the forests for a wide range of values and uses. Forests moderate climate; protect hill slopes from soil erosion and landslides by providing protective cover and mechanical support to top soils; improve air and water quality by serving as a stabilizing factor for the atmosphere both regarding moisture and carbondioxide contents, taking rain water under the upper surface of the land through inward transportation and provide habitat for countless species of plants and animals. They also offer a multitude of recreational opportunities that are enjoyed by us. Further, by providing fodder, fuel, timber, and raw material for different forest-based industries forests sustain the economies of thousands of communities across the world.

Our awareness of the imprtance of forests to the global environment is changing the future of forest management around the world. Over the past decade, forests have emerged as a major consideration in Global discussion on sustainable development. Since, the United Nation's Earth Submit held in Rio de Janeiro, Brazil, in 1992, remarkable progress has been made in advancing the worldwide consensus on addressing forest issues. At the same time, an increasing number of countries are viewing their forests as a source of economic wealth and development. The International community recognizes the multiple benefits and roles of forests. Given the wide disparities between countries in forest ecosystems and social and economic priorities, finding a common definition of what constitutes sustainable forest management is crucial.

Owing to the tremendous increase in the human and livestock population in many parts of the globe, rapid industrial development and fast urban growth, the forest ecosystems in underdeveloped, developing, as well as in the developed regions of the world have come under increased biotic stress during the last few decades. Consequent upon this, the forest resources have been depleting and degrading fast throughout the world. Besides, road construction, mining and quarrying and extension of cultivation have contributed significantly to the degradation of forests in many regions, particularly in the developing and underdeveloped countries of the world. Consequently, a process of rapid degradation of forest resources is now under operation even in the high mountains and other ecologically fragile ecosystems of our planet.

The paper here is devoted to a study of forestry in the province of British Columbia in Canada in the light of these emerging issues in regard to forestry. It is split into six parts. Part one gives an overview of forest resources in British Columbia. The second part discusses traditional resource use of forestry. Part three examines the environmental impact of commercial forestry. Parts four and five deal with the economic and social impacts respectively of this commercial use. The concluding part brings together the main inferences of the study.

FOREST RESOURCES OF BRITISH COLUMBIA

Canada is one of the few developed nations of the world still richly endowed with large areas of natural forests covering 453.30 million ha of land surface of the country which accounts for 45.47 percent of the country's geographical area (Table 1). The vast forest resource of Canada has been integral to the development of the country as a nation and to its culture, traditions and history. Of the 453.30 million hectares of forests in Canada, 57 percent are considered commercial forests-capable of producing a range of both timber and non-timber benefits. However, 50 per cent of these forests are currently accessible and managed for timber production (Council of Forest Industries, 1994, Statistics Canada, 1994). Canada is unique in that the vast majority of forests (94 per cent) are publicly owned. On behalf of the public, provincial governments manage 71 percent, while the federal and territorial governments manage approximately 23 percent of the forestland in the country. The remaining 6 per cent of the forests are privately owned by 42,5000 landowners across Canada (Table 1). Forest management in Canada is a matter of provincial jurisdiction, and each province has its own set of legislation, policies and regulations governing forest activities within its borders (Ministry of Forests, Government of Canada, 1996).

British Columbia with a forest area of 60.30 million ha, contains as much as 49.20 per cent of natural forests of Canada. The forests account for a large part of British Columbia. The majority of forests are coniferous forests. The province encompasses a geographical land surface of 94.80 million hectares. Fresh water lakes and rivers cover 2 million hectares leaving about 93 million hectares for terra firma (Farley, 1979). Out of this, about 60.30 million hectares, or nearly two-third, is forestland. The Ministry of forests classifies 46 million hectares as productive forestland, and defines 26 million hectares of these as being 'productive and available' (Ministry of Forests, British Columbia, 1991 and 1996). Generally speaking, the forests of British Columbia cover more area than the entire state of California (41.1 million hectares) or Washington or Oregon combined (42.8 million hectares). The forest area classified as productive and available is slightly more than the state of Oregon. In total, the province forests contain 7 percent of the world's stock of softwood timber and 45 percent of Canada's or roughly speaking, about 8 billion cubic metres. The hardwood inventory of 650 million cubic metres is much less significant, being 1.8 per cent of the world stock and 12.2 percent of the Canadian total (Schwindt and Heaps, 1996).

The forestland base in the province is not only immense; it is also extremely varied. The forests of British Columbia are essential to the survival of many plants, animals and other organisms. More than 200000 species, representing two-thirds of all the species found in the province are dependent on forest habitats (British Columbia, Ministry of Forests, 1995). In British Columbia, the complex interplay of climatic control is such as to produce climatic diversity greater than in any other part of Canada. Accordingly, the distribution of forest resource, both in species composition and in per hectare volume, shows marked regional differentiation, the contrasts from coast to interior and from lower to higher elevations being particularly strong (Farley, 1972). Canada has been divided up into eight types of forest regions, five of which are found in British Columbia- the Boreal, Coast, Columbia, Montane, and Sub alpine forest regions (Rowe, 1972). The province has an estimated 8 million hectares of Coastal forests. Of these, 5.25 million hectares are covered by trees of over 120 years old. The dominant species are hemlock, cedar, Balsam Douglas fir, and the true firs. In the interior, lodgepole pine and spruce growing in montane and sub-alpine regions comprise the larger part of the accessible timber resource (Farley, 1972).

FOREST AND TRADITIONAL RESOURCE USE STRUCTURE

The forests of British Columbia have sustained the economy and culture of hundreds of traditional forest dependent communities across the province, and the timber they provide has been a driving force of the provincial economy for more than a century. A broad range of values are associated with British Columbia's forests – biodiversity, community stability, gathering, geo-climatic grazing, heritage, hunting, recreation, science and education, socio-political, spiritual and aesthetic, timber, tourism, water etc. (British Columbia, Ministry of Forests, 1995). But, traditionally, timber has been considered as the only important value of forests in British Columbia. It has been widely proclaimed that fifty cents out of every dollar spent in British Columbia is generated by forest industry. The validity of this statement is hard to deny. As a source of employment and as a generator of net production value, the primary and secondary phases of forest utilization far exceed their counterparts in other resource-based industries of the province. Regionally, the relative importance of forest-based industries as producer of income and employment varies somewhat, but even in the areas of greatest industrial diversity and in those few where agriculture or mining are dominant, forestry is a very significant sector of the economy (Farley, 1972). Even today, with increased emphasis on multiple use and protection of other values associated with the forests, the timber remains the most important forest resource, and the commercial forests sector is the dominant user of this natural resource (Commission on Resources and Environment, 1995)

The commercial forest sector manages forests, extracts timber, and converts wood fiber into products. The commercial sector activities fall into two divisions: forestry and manufacturing. The forestry division consists of two industry groups: logging and forestry services. Within the manufacturing division there are two industry groups that use wood fiber as a primary input: the wood industries group and the paper and allied industries group. The commercial forest sector accounts for 8 per cent of Gross Domestic Product and about 6 percent of the provincial employment. Out of the total wealth generated by the sector, labour's share accounts for 67 per cent, enterprises receive 27 per cent and the Crown captures only about 6 percent (Hamilton, 1996).

As discussed in the preceding section, forestry is the main segment of British Columbia' economy. Commercial logging started in southwestern corner of the province, in 1840's when permanent European settlements emerged in Vancouver island (Robinson, 1972). But it was not until the early 1850s, when external trade linkages from Victoria to overseas markets began to develop, that logging became a significant sector in the colonial economy. Sites of early logging were close to tidewater where trees could be felled and limbed, then slid to water from where they could be floated to the point of manufacturing. During the early years, logging operations were confined to the southern Vancouver Island where the evolution and growth of agricultural settlements began and no commercial exploitation was made of the vast forest resources of the mainland. The discovery of placer gold along the alluvial bars of the lower Fraser river, and subsequently along the tributary streams in the interior, gave tremendous stimulus to the colonial economy and resulted in a basic reorientation of settlements, and by mid- 1860s commercial forestry had extended to the mainland, particularly along the shores of Burrard Inlets (Farley, 1972)

By 1990, logging was rather widely dispersed in the Vancouver area,.along the lower mainland coast, and along the east coastal plain of Vancouver Island. During the first quarter of the last century, commercial forestry emerged as the linchpin of the provincial economy and the pattern of logging activity expanded along both the margin of the Strait of Georgia northward to the northern end of Vancouver Island. Logging continued to be spatially associated with saw milling but the introduction of newer means of log transport permitted a greater separation, so that logging camps were established at some distance from milling sites. The combination of amenable topography, quality and volume of timber stands, coupled with the introduction of steam engine and logging railway, facilitated the process of this separation. This growing spatial dissociation contributed significantly to the development of large capacity with fixed mills that could draw upon a large resource hinterland for continuing logging operations and this trend has continued to the present (Farley, 1972).

ENVIRONMENTAL IMPACTS OF COMMERCIAL FORESTRY SECTOR

Since, a significant number of rural communities and a large proportion of provincial economy depend heavily upon the commercial forest sector, which accounts for 8 percent of GDP and 6 percent of provincial employment, the demand for timber has been increasing constantly for the last 10-15 years. This has facilitated reckless exploitation of forests in British Columbia, resulting in the degradation of natural environment, devastation of the economy and culture of a large number of traditional communities, and decline in forest sector economy in the province. Empirical studies carried out in British Columbia reveal that indiscriminate deforestation (200000 ha/year) and construction of logging roads have adversely affected the hydrological cycle of watersheds resulting in the destruction of fish and wildlife habitats, accelerated soil erosion and landslides, pollution of water sources and loss of biodiversity and wilderness in the entire province (Figure 1).

As a result, the forest resources have depleted and eroded steadily and significantly bringing about rapid changes in the natural environment and biodiversity of the region. British Columbia is a mountainous province and most of its geographical area lies in high Rocky and Coastal Mountain ranges which are among the youngest and recent mountain systems of the earth. Consequently, these vast mountain tracts are geologically unstable and ecologically vulnerable (Robinson, 1991). The unabated devastation of forest resources in British Columbia has disrupted the fragile ecosystem of the watersheds through reduced water recharge, increased surface run-off, accelerated erosion, and destruction of wilderness and wildlife in the province. The indiscriminate clear-cutting of natural forests over large areas and construction of logging roads for the transportation of timber from remote forests to main roads and rail heads have promoted the processes of slope failure and mass movement resulting in massive landslides and mudslides along the fragile mountain slopes. The effects of poor logging and road building practices are clearly visible along the steep wet slopes of fragile mountains in the region. It was observed that it takes about 7 to 20 years for the big roots of tree stumps to rot out and the massive landslides to begin to occur on steep slopes. But, steep slope logging, still legal under British Columbia's Forest Practices Code, is happening all over the province, particularly along ecologically vulnerable pacific coast. Hundreds of miles of shoreline have been degraded by the clear-cut which have turned some of the most beautiful coastlines in the world into some of the despoiled ones (Power, 1995).

Everyday, timber companies operate thousands of logging trucks in hundreds of remote valleys, destroying an irreplaceable and priceless natural heritage of the world. In the high elevation, steep sloped valleys are being clear-cut to the river edge and dragging logs across them. Even, the last of Canada's very best remaining ancient temperate old growth rainforests are being clear-cut on B.C.'s isolated Rain coasts. In addition to this, the New Forest Practices Code encourages the dispersal of smaller clear-cuts over a larger area, resulting in many more clear-cuts and logging roads causing more damage to the fragile natural environment of the region. Clear cutting of forests along the ocean shore is a logging practice still approved under B.C.'s New Forest Practice Code. Most of the beautiful valleys along the Rain Coast are now the ravaged domains of commercial forestry operations. Over the next few years, several such natural heritage watersheds are scheduled to be completely deforested.

Accelerated Erosion and Landslides

The forests on mountain slopes are particularly fragile and large-scale denudation might lead to severe soil erosion process and massive landslides along the hill slopes. The effects of poor logging and road-building practices on the steep wet slopes of Slocan Valley are now clearly visible. For example, in the Frog Peak area of Slocan Valley, the clear-cut slopes are marred by massive landslides and mass wasting. There have been major landslides into Lemon Creek, slides into Slocan River, Crescent Valley and into Airy Creek due to logging operations and road building, during the recent years. Similarly, in the north end of Slocan Valley, there have been massive logging related landslides into Dennis, Wilson and Silverton Creeks (Slocan Valley Watershed Alliance, 1997).

The Geo-Hydrological Imbalances

A significant amount of water that drains into most of the mountain-rivers in British Columbia is subsurface water. About 30 years back Slaymaker (1972) pointed towards significant changes in mean as well as extreme discharges, timing of discharge events, sediment discharges, and water quality of six major river basins in British Columbia which represent major perturbations in the regional natural environment due to rapid land use change including large scale deforestation in the province. The degradation of natural vegetation, particularly, in headwaters of streams causes irreparable damage to the geo-hydrology of the region by reducing the amount of infiltration through which numerous springs, streams, channels and lakes receive their water.

The creek headwaters which are characterized by slow-flowing small streams and wetlands, and are usually located on the top of the ridges, feed into the steeper, low elevation-creeks where hundreds of rural communities get their water. Disturbance, such as, clear-cutting and road construction, on the creek, directly influences the discharge and volume of water flow, the seasonal temperature variation, and presence of harmful bacteria in the water. During recent years, it was observed that the level of sedimentation in Slocan River increased dramatically during rainstorms due to logging related landslides into Lemon Creek. The clear cutting of steep wet mountain slopes has already caused great disturbances to the sub-surface hydrology of the region, and consequently, increased the risk to the settlements and highways in the area. In view of these distrubances in subsurface water regime, the Ministry of Environment, Government of B.C. had to issue a flood warning for British Columbia in the spring of 1997. The hydrological investigations carried out in New Denver Flats, Perry Ridge, Elliot Anderson and Hasty Creek valleys of the province during a dry spell revealed that these areas are extremely wet even during dry years and major floods and mudslides may occur if mid and high elevation logging of the headwaters of these sensitive areas proceeded (Slocan Valley Watershed Alliance, 1997).

Studies carried out in Anderson-Christian-Trozzo Watershed Complex revealed that the region receives water from countless small seeps, springs, and small intermediate creeks from which hundreds of communities draw their domestic water. The land is steep and the soils are unstable, and the creeks flow in steep narrow channels. The water of these channels becomes heavily polluted due to increased sedimentation owing to logging induced landslides and mudslides. When the water levels rise in the streams, they begin carrying rocks and minerals from the slides downstream and into domestic water system. The hydrologists based on the study of these watersheds strongly warned that these channels should not be crossed by roads because they are highly fragile and represent too much risk of damage of the downstream water users systems. These drainages are too small to manage for both water quality and timber production (Slocan Valley Watershed Alliance, 1997).

Loss of Wilderness and Wildlife

Due to indiscriminate plunder of natural vegetation in B.C., Canada's great old-growth forests and roadless wilderness areas are disappearing at an ever-increasing rate

(Schwindt and Heaps, 1996). For example, on the eastern shores of the Pacific Ocean, along the mainland coast of British Columbia lies the last great extent of ancient temperate rainforest left in the world. Bounded by the high and rugged coastal mountains, it has the deepest and longest Fiords in the world. With its islands, beaches, bears and wild Salmon, this region has rich wilderness and biodiversity to equal the grandest parks in the world. The Rainforest, over 600-km long, with more than still pristine rainforest valleys, is home of first nations, grizzly bears, wolves and more than 1000 distinct species of wild salmon. The fate of its never logged rain forested valleys; the largest of this ecosystem left on the world is rapidly becoming the focus of major international conservation movements. The goal of these great conservation compaigns is to save the wilderness and biological diversity of the region from devastation through timber extraction. But it has upto now, been explored more by people seeking their fortune from the rich timber extraction than those relishing its wilderness state. Since 1990, some 14 pristine rainforest valleys over 5000 hectares in size have been roaded and logged completely along the B.C. Raincoast. This represents a loss of more than two wild river valleys a year (Raincoast Conservation Society, 1997). The timber companies know where the best of timber is found and target it first. They barge in the bulldozers, punch logging roads into the hearts of virgin river valleys, log out the ancient legacy of stumps, eroding fragile mountain slopes and biologically bankrupt the untouched wilderness. The forest companies will be long gone before the consequences of their devastation and destruction in the remote fiords and inlets of British Columbia's Rainforests are discovered and assessed. This large scale devastation of natural ecosystem cannot be justified by a few short-term logging jobs to native population, and a short-term forestry development working plan cannot chart the future for a ten thousand year old intact ecosystem that could support eco-tourism ventures and clean rivers full of fish that would employ and feed thousands of communities indefinitely (Western Canada Wilderness Committee, 1997).

The Conservationists have identified two areas that must be protected – the Greater Bear Rainforest and the Stoltmann Wilderness. The great Bear Rainforest, with its large pristine valleys is comprised of three areas-The Greater Ecstall Region in the north, the Right Inlet Region in the south, and a large Mid Coast wilderness region including the Spirit Bear Park Proposal, sandwiched in between. The Stoltmann Wilderness area, a microcosm of wild natural world, encompasses 260,000 hectares landscape in the pristine headwaters of the Squeamish and Lillooet River Systems – the Sims, Clendenning, Upper Elaho and Upper Lillooet valleys. Together, these four contiguous valleys make up half of all the unlogged valleys over 5000 hectares left in the entire 4.2 million-hectare Lower Mainland region. The region is characterized by timeless landscape of Douglas fir and ancient red cedar forests, flower filled meadows, pristine rivers, abundant fish, eagles, moose, grizzly bear, mountain goats and wolves. The Stoltmann wilderness is a rich mosaic of old growth forests, alpine meadows, marshes and wetlands, rivers and glaciers. All together it is a lot of ideal fish and wildlife habitat. B.C. government biologists have estimated the numbers of some of the large wildlife species inhabiting the Stoltmann Wilderness at 8 grizzly bear, 700 black bear, 55 moose, 240 mountain goats, 8 wolves and 15 cougars (Western Canada Wilderness Committee, 1997). This is a wildlife roll call unequalled by any provincial park in the Lower Mainland. Besides, the Stoltmann Wilderness also contains a number of species made rare by habitat destruction elsewhere. The extraordinary variety of wildlife found in the Stoltmann Wilderness should come as no surprise. After all, the Stoltmann wilderness is the biggest wild area with the largest extent of old growth forests left on the B.C.'s coast. There are many outstanding trees found in the Stoltmann, including some of the last large groves of old growth Douglas fir left on the B.C. coast. Many of trees are over 1000 years old. It is easy to forget that just 200-km southeast away live over 2 million people in one of North America's major urban centre – Vancouver. Despite its inestimable ecological and recreation values, the Stoltmann Wilderness is increasingly threatened by logging. Logging roads, bridges and clear cuts are already approved in the area for coming years. The forests are already fast running out in Southwest British Columbia, and the Stoltmann old growth forests are coveted by powerfull multinational timber companies, such as, timber union giants International Forests Products (InterFor), International Wood Workers of America (IWA) and the provincial government that seeks social appeasement rather than ecological and community sustainability (Raincoast Conservation Society, 1997).

Grizzly bears on the Rain Coast need clusters of wild-forested valleys to survive. Most of their food is old growth related and dependent. They use the ancient forests for protection from heat and cold and for safe hiding and denning. There are no grizzly sanctuaries offering adequate long-term protection for grizzly bears on the entire B.C. coast. The widespread logging operation in the region is eventually leading to the demise of this northern grizzly bear population in the region. Clear cuts and logging roads devastate the natural habitats and create the problem of survival for old-growth dependent grizzlies. B.C. Government has just approved further logging in a number of prime grizzly bear-salmon valleys. Besides, as mentioned above, the inevitable siltation of rivers precipitated by massive alteration and erosion of the landscape is killing wild slamon. Salmon are principal food for the bears, especially during the fall of summers when they prepare for hibernation (Raincoast Conservation Society, 1997).

Damage to Fish and Fish Habitats

Each species has special environmental requirements for shelter, food and reproduction. Every physiographic, climatic and vegetation zone has distinctive fauna associated with it. The smaller animals are distributed according to vegetation zones, but some large predators, such as, wolf have a broad geographical distribution. Fish and wildlife provide the cornerstone of hunting Indian cultures in the entire Pacific Northwest. Salmon is a staple in the diet of coastal communities, and also plays an important part in the commercial and religious life of the local groups. The salmon family includes steelhead, trout's and char, as well as five species common to the West Coast: Coho, sockeye, pink, chum and spring.

The pacific salmon are anadromous, they breed and spend part of their lives in freshwater before travelling to the ocean where they feed untill maturity. The salmon are born from eggs laid in gravel beds of streams some 15 to 1500 km away from the sea. They feed and grow in lakes and rivers upto a year or more. Then during the spring freshet, they head downstream to the sea, where they feed and grow. After sometime the salmon migrate back to their home streams, struggling up to the spawning areas where they were born. The salmon stop feeding once they enter freshwater and die soon after spawning. The thousands of small stream in British Columbia sustain the majority of fish, particularly the salmon. As described above, streams provide living, feeding and spawning areas for fish. All salmonids need an adequate flow of clean and cool water. A good rearing stream should have different types of habitat to provide cover for fish, such as, pools, forest debris, boulders and gravels, overhanging trees and bush; a constant flow of clean water, moderate summer temperatures, few predators, and lots of insects for food. In a good spawning stream, adult salmonids should be able to reach spawning gravels that have free flowing silt free water.

Salmon are highly sensitive to environmental changes, particularly water quality and flow. Salmon habitats and spawning beds in British Columbia are now being badly damaged due to heavy siltation caused by indiscriminate logging and construction of logging roads, in stream watersheds. Thus, the inevitable siltation of rivers precipitated by massive alteration and erosion of landscape is killing salmon in all major streams. The biologically rich river valleys and their sheltering ancient forests are critical in maintaining the salmon. The river valleys have prime grizzly bear habitats and provide most beautiful anchorages on the whole coast. But, many multinational Timber Companies like Western Forests Products have forest cutting rights to the forests of the area. In British Columbia and Yukon territory, scientists have recently documented the extinction of 142 salmon stocks, and classified 624 more slamon stocks at high risk due to a century of commercial forestry operations in these provinces of Canada (Western Canada Wilderness Committee, 1997).

ECONOMIC IMPLICATONS OF COMMERCIAL FORESTRY SECTOR

Extraction of forest – based resources, such as, timber, fish, trapping, ranching, tourism etc., generates economic activity that sustains communities. It is noteworthy here that in British Columbia, a significant number of rural communities primarily depend heavily upon the commercial forest sector for employment. In order to examine the community dependence on commercial forestry sector, studies were carried in 63 local areas which include 441 individual communities in the province (Schwindt and Heaps, 1996). The results of the investigation revealed that out of 63, 19 local areas, comprising 141 rural communities were dependent on the commercial forestry for 25 per cent or more of their basic income (Table–2). Commercial forestry operations generate income that is distributed to the timber owner (the Crown), labour and the owner of industry or timber companies, and entrepreneurs working in the sector. These recipients spend that income and this has effects, through multipliers, on economic activity, from the local to the international levels (Hayter and Galois, 1991). At the local level, it plays and important role in sustaining the local communities through creating direct as well as indirect employment in the various sectors of forest industry. In the early sixties, the commercial forestry sector contributed about 2 billion dollars to provincial Gross Domestic Products that accounted for 15 per cent of the total GDP. But, in 1994, it contributed 5 billion dollars, which is now only 7.5 per cent of total GDP. The forestry jobs have declined and the economic spin-off benefits from the commercial forestry have also reduced drastically (Hamilton, 1996; Schwindt. And Heaps, 1996).

This shows that employment in the forest sector has declined from 100000 at the beginning of 1980s to just 85000 today. Although the forest harvest levels have increased dramatically between 1970 and 1993, jobs per 1000 cubic metre wood harvested fell by 30 percent (Schwindt and Heaps, 1997). Studies carried in the province cast serious doubt on repeated forest industry and government's claim that the provinces forest sector creates hundreds of thousands of jobs. Far from being generators of new and spin-off jobs, major sectors of the industry continue to find new ways of increasing the efficiency of production by replacing people with machines. This decrease in the proportion of the workforce, while the forests of the province continue to be over cut, is the high price of efficiency. Logging rates climbed steadily yet the number of jobs generated from an increasing cut did not keep pace. As the time progressed, far fewer people were employed for each tree logged. Despite clear-cutting the valleys and vulnerable mountain slopes at mushrooming logging rates, which reached a record high of 90 million cubic metres of wood at the end of 1980s, total direct employment in the forest industry today has not increased from 85000 jobs (Schwindt and Heaps, 1997).

Efficiency has not been the only cause of job loss in commercial forestry sector. The most important reason for decline in forest-based jobs is that after the intensive logging of old growth forests began, projected logging decreased (Figure. 1). Today the annual logging rate in the province is around 71 million cubic metres, which clears about 200000 hectares of forests annually. As the available hectares of old growth forests shrinks, the rate will soon fall to as low as 50 million cubic metres from clearing the area of same size (Figure. 1). The second growth forests are for the most part still too young to cut, even when mature, they match old growth neither in quality nor in quantity. When the forests are logged so quickly, future-logging rates inevitably fall, and as the logging rates fall there will be continued depletion of forests as well as the loss of jobs (Figure. 1). The annual logging rates are falling continuously (from 70 in 1995 to 50 million cubic metres in 1997) owing to complete exploitation of old-growth forests, which has resulted in steady decline in commercial forest sector employment and revenue to the Crown. The forest industry continues to argue that this looming shortfall in timber supplies results from efforts to protect the few remaining unlogged watersheds from forestry operations. But the fact is that today the industry retains access to almost all the working forests it held 10 years ago. This brings out the fact clearly that the future productivity of forest industry in B.C. as well as the sustainability of forest dependent communities depends on the intact biodiversity of the forests. If the unlogged forests of the province are indeed to be given the protection required to maintain this biodiversity, as opposed to the minimal protection they have received to date, there will inevitably be downward pressure on jobs (Schwindt and Heaps, 1997).

SOCIAL IMPACT

Impact on Community Sustainability

In addition to a large number of rural communities that depend on commercial forestry sector, a significant number of people, particularly, the native population still depends of the extraction of primary forest resources in British Columbia. Due to intensive logging and massive loss of biodiversity, the sustainability of rural communities is collapsing through the depletion of primary forest resources that support traditional economic activities, such as gathering, grazing, fishing, hunting, ranching etc. It was observed during field investigations that a large number of native families inhabiting the forest areas of British Columbia are now being forced to leave their traditional forest-based means of livelihood, and migrate out of their homes in search of alternative means of sustaining. In some areas, the local forest dependent communities have started a series of movements against loss of environment and biodiversity due to unabated logging operations in the province.

Loss of Aboriginal Culture and Traditional Ecological Knowledge

With the deprivation of traditional economic activities, the Native communities are also losing their culture and indigenous knowledge developed through several thousand years, which has a great implications to community sustainability and conservation and management of natural resources (Figure. 1). Canada has a large segment of population defined as natives or Aboriginal. The traditional resource use pattern of native communities in Canada is closely interlinked with the forests, rangelands, water bodies and wilderness, which are of prime importance for the sustenance of these traditional societies in the country. The aboriginal communities in Canada are, in general, more conservation-oriented and follow certain basic moral guidelines required for mutual co-existence with mother nature.

These values of sustainability are deeply rooted in the aboriginal culture and traditions that are based on the concept of rational use of natural resources, collective survival and social equity. Consequently, there is a symbiotic relationship between the natural environment and the resource use practices, that permitted hundreds of traditional communities across the province to survive in reasonable harmony with nature for the last several hundred years. Owing to the depletion of forests, wildlife habitats and biodiversity, the aboriginal communities in British Columbia, have been forced to change their lifestyle, traditions and the traditional resource use practices. As a result, the indigenous knowledge and cultural values that contributed significantly to the achievement of resource sustainability and community building have eroded steadily and significantly. This is a loss not merely because we need these communities as curious momentos of human history to be preserved but because their practical experience with nature is a part of human heritage that can help significantly to point appropriate ways to the conservation of environment and sustainable development of natural resources in British Columbia.

INFERENCES

Despite the increasing realization and growing public concern regarding the conservation of forests, biodiversity and wilderness, the forest resources of British Columbia continue to be exploited mainly for commercial benefits. As a result, the critical components of natural environment, such as, land, water and biodiversity are being depleted and degraded, and the community sustainability is affected. Consequently, there is increasing demand for the withdrawal of forest-lands from commercial timber extraction, within the province. The rationale for these demands include watershed protection, habitat conservation, protection and conservation of other natural resources, such as, water and fish stocks, and the establishment of wilderness preserves. It is therefore, high time to make radical changes in the current forest management policies and forest industry. The new management policy must begin with evolving a comprehensive and sustainable land-use framework for the entire province, and forest management must be treated as one of the essential components of overall land-use policy. The main emphasis should be on the conservation of biodiversity which is the source of future productivity. There should be increased public participation in the forest management and community control of the forest industry so that more employment could be generated through promoting more labour-oriented and value added manufacturing, and the forests could be protected for future generations.

Table 1: The Forest Resource

Resource Parametres	Canada	British Columbia
Total Area (Million hectares)	997.00	94.80
Forest land (Million hectares)	453.30	60.30
Forest land (Percent of total land)	45.47	63.61
Softwood Stock (Billion Cubic Metres)	17.80	8.30
Percent of World Softwood Stock	15.60	07.00
Provincial Ownership of Forest Land (Percent)	71.00	95.00
Federal Ownership of forest Land (Percent)	23.00	01.00
Private Ownership of Forest Land (Percent)	06.00	04.00
Annual Allowable Timber Harvest (Million Cubic Metres)	229.80	72.40
Annual Harvest Area (Ha)	988960.00	**190244.00**

Table 2: Community Dependence on the Commercial Forestry in British Columbia

Local Area	Dependence on Commercial Forestry Sector (in Percent)	Number of Communities
(1)	(2)	(3)
Quesnel	39	10
Hazelton	39	07
North Thompson	37	08
Port hardy	37	08
Vanderhoof	35	06
Powell River	35	08
Lake Cowichan	35	04
Mcbride-Valemount	33	04
Burns lake	33	04
Golden	33	03
Campwell River	33	10
Alberni	31	06

(1)	(2)	(3)
Prince George	30	06
Fort Nelson	29	02
Williams Lake	27	20
Smithers-Houston	26	08
Queen Charlotte Islands	26	07
Castlegar Arrow Lakes	25	16
Lillooet	25	04

Source: Schwindt and Heaps (1996), Chopping up the Money Tree, The David Suzuki foundation, Vancover, British Columbia, Canada.

ENVIRONMENTAL AND SOCIO-ECONOMIC IMPLICATIONS OF COMMERCIAL FORESTRY IN BRITISH COLUMBIA, CANADA

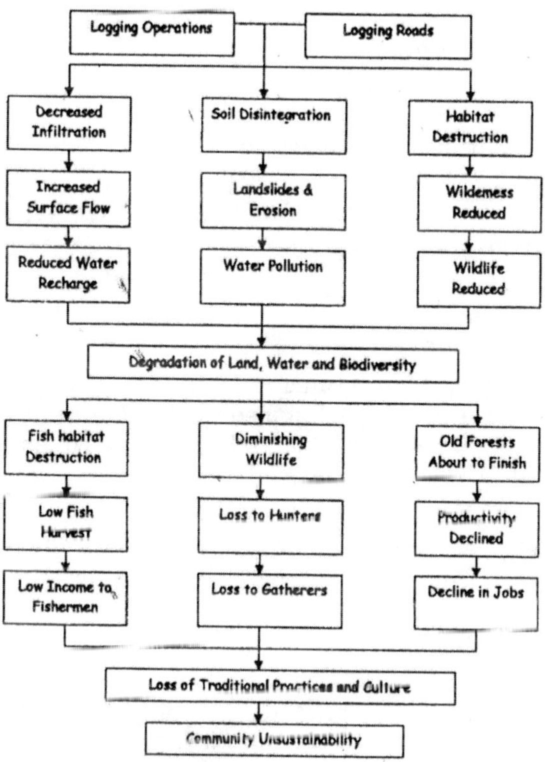

References

British Columbia, Ministry of Forests (1995), *Forest, Range and Recreation Analysis,* Victoria: Crown Publications.

Commission on Resources and Environment (1995), British Columbia's Sustainability Strategy, *Report to the Legislative Assembly,* 1994-95.

Council of Forest Industries (1994), *British Columbia Forest Industry Book*, Vancouver.

Farley, A.L. (1972), *The Forest Resource of British Columbia*, pp.87-118, University of Toronto Press, Toronto.

Hamilton, G. (1996), Victoria Close to Forest Industry Conflict, Suzuki Foundation Claims, *Sun Forestry Reporter,* June 21 1997, Vancouver.

Hayter, R. and Galois, R. (1991), The Wheel of Fortune: British Columbia's Lumber and the Global Economy, in Paul M. Koroscil (ed). *British Columbia: Geographical Essays*, pp. 169-202, Department of Geography, Simon Fraser University, Burnaby, British Columbia.

Ministry of Forests, Government of Canada (1991), *The State of Canada's Forests*, Ottawa.

Power, T.M. (1995), Economic Well Being and Environmental Protection in the Pacific Northwest – *Consensus Report* by Pacific Northwest Economists, December 1995, Mimeo.

Raincoats Conservation Society (1997), *Educational Report*, May 1997, Vancouver.

Robinson, J.L. (1972), Areal Pattern and Regional Character of British Columbia, in J. Lewis Robinson (ed). *Studies in Canadian Geography.* British Columbia, pp 1-8, University of Toronto Press, Toronto.

Robinson, J.L. (1991), Geographical Regions of British Columbia, in Paul M. Koroscil (ed.) *British Columbia: Geographical Essays*, pp. 19-40, Department of Geography, Simon Fraser University, Burnaby, British Columbia.

Rowe, J.S. (1972), *Forest Regions of Canada*, Information Canada, Ottawa.

Schwindt, R. and Heaps, T. (1996), Chopping up the Money Tree: Distributing the Wealth from *British Columbia's Forests*, Report to the David Suzuki Foundation, Vancouver, Canada.

Slaymaker, O. (1972), Physiography and Hydrology of Six River basins of British Columbia, in J.Lewis Robinson ed. Studies in Canadian Geography: *British Columbia*, pp.32-68, University of Toronto Press, Toronto.

Slocan Valley Watershed Alliance (1997), *News Letter*, Spring, 1997, Vancouver

Statistics Canda (1997), Ottawa.

Western Canada Wilderness Committee (1997), *Educational Report,* Vol. 16 No.4 summer 1997, Vancouver.

Joint Forest Management

5

Vanita Suneja

JFM in the context of Forestry in India

The forests lands in India are administered by the state governments. How will the products from the forest be used? By whom and under what conditions forests may be accessed? What kind of technical systems are to be adapted to harvest, regenerate, plant or protect forests? The decisions on all these matters, legally lies with the State governments which manage forest through their administrative arm known as the Forest Department. However, the State government is not allowed to divert the forest land for non-forestry purposes such as agriculture, horticulture, mining, housing etc. without the permission of Central government, which has a specific Ministry for this known as Ministry of Environment and Forests (MoEF). Forestry became a concurrent subject in India in 1976.

Forestlands are a monopoly of the government and had been a source of revenue for the government, but at the same time, millions of people who are dependent on forests for their livelihood and a number of Industrial houses who need forests to create wealth, claim their respective stakes on forest produce and forest lands. The government has acknowledged these claims but delimit these claims on behalf of the claim of the general public (national and international, present and future generations) on fresh air and water, which are functions of forest eco systems. Hence the recurrent tone of the current forest policy(1988) is of conservation. Apart from conservation, governments also acknowledge the claim of wildlife, represented by wildlife enthusiasts. The proxy representation of claims is not only limited to wildlife but is spread to other claims also, like the claims of forest dependent people as voiced by groups of people, who could be categorized as Social activists, NGO/Civil society, Developmental organizations and foundations. Similarly claims of industry are also voiced by financial institutions, business confederations and, lately by development organizations also. Which claim gets priority over others at a particular time is determined by the relative power of the respective claimants and their supportive groups on the policy field.

In view of the conflicting claims on a single resource and continuous degradation of forest resource over a period of 100 years, many changes in policies took place. The policy shift in 1988 forest policy compared to the earlier forest policies, was in favour of the rural community living in the vicinity of forest (see Inbox 1). The policy actors working for the support of reforms in forest public domain were eventually able to crack the monopolistic control of the forest department on the forestland. The oppressed rural communities were enabled to legitimately access the forest. An effort was made to create space for the involvement of communities in the forest. The reluctance and opposition to this change by the forest department was apparent in internal departmental and public discourses.

The concept of people's participation, and the phenomena of large foreign funding to support forestry projects were already in vogue ever since the time of the introduction of Social forestry. But Social forestry was an attempt in 1970's and 80's to wean away the dependence of people on government forestland by growing plantations on various kinds of private and common lands other than forestland. On the other hand, the change in forest Policy in 1988 helped in pushing the idea of recognizing community efforts in the protection of natural forest area itself. This was quite threatening to the hold of Forest Department in forest area. A strategy was adopted to gain government legitimacy for grassroots initiatives by Ford Foundation program officers , working in conjunction with selected senior foresters, government planners and NGOs leaders to develop a series of case studies documenting community forest protection system and at the same time casting these as a "partnership" between forest departments and communities and labelled it as "JOINT FOREST MANAGEMENT"(JFM). This reassured foresters that they would retain some oversight control over how forest would be utilized (Poffenberger, 1995). The first resolution for JFM was passed by the State of Orissa in 1988, followed by West Bengal in 1989. Subsequently in 1991, several senior NGO leaders and retired civil servants drafted guidelines for a ministerial resolution supporting a national JFM program.

For the last 10 years Joint Forest Management, emerged as a concept, as a government order, as a programme and as a management tool, all terms currently being used interchangeably. It does not imply that the whole forest area has been covered under JFM. Out of the 63.73 million ha of geographical area under forest, the JFM is operational in 10.25 million ha of forest, that constitutes only 16 % of the total forest area.

1894 Forest Policy

"It should be remembered that subject to certain conditions to be referred to presently, the claims of cultivation are stronger than claims of forest preservation... Accordingly, wherever an effective demand for cultivable land exists and can only be supplied from forest area, the land should ordinarily be relinquished without hesitation"(GoI 1894)

1952 Forest Policy

" The accident of a village being situated close to the forest does't prejudice the rights of the country as a whole to receive the benefits of a national asset"(GoI 1952)

1988 Forest Policy

"The life of tribal and other poor living within and near forests revolves around forests. The rights and concessions enjoyed by them should be fully protected. Their domestic requirements of fuelwood, fodder, minor forest produce and construction timber should be the *first charge* (emphasis added) on forest produce" (*ibid*)

The **forest cover** of the country, as per the present assessment, is 63.73 million ha constituting 19.39% of the geographic area of the country out of which 37.74 million ha (11.48 %) is dense forest, 25.50 million ha(7.76%) open forest and 0.49 million ha (0.15%) mangroves. ***source: FSI 1999.***

JFM recognizes the claim for direct access to forest and forest produce of the **nearby forest dependent community** and the **forest Department**. Where are the other claimants like Industries and Wildlife enthusiasts? The policy and situation before the 1982 Forest Conservation Act was very conducive for Industry to get direct access to forest by taking large forest areas on long lease at concessional rates from the respective State governments. The 1982 Act put some restrictions on the leasing of forestland. The situation became more difficult for the Industry after 1988 Forest Policy, which has totally denied direct access to Industry in forest for raw material but suggests that raw material should be grown by Industries on private land on its own or through farmers. On the wildlife front, a number of national parks and sanctuaries have been created after 1970. The FSI 1999 reports that there are 87 national parks and 484 wildlife sanctuaries with total areas of 4.0 million ha and 11.54 million ha respectively. These together constitute 15.6 million ha and form 4.74% of the geographical area of the country. In addition, 11 biosphere reserves have also been created with a geographical area of 4.3 million ha. So far, implementation of JFM has been kept outside the domain of protected areas.

Strategies adopted by the conservationist for bringing more and more area under protected area domain and the strategies being adopted by the industries to get entrance in forest areas are beyond the realm of this discussion paper. Albeit, the idea is to draw attention to the whole canvas of forest sustainability by positioning the remaining actors in the background.

JFM in principle and action

The concept of Joint Forest Management was constructed to meet the challenge of forest degradation. The learnings of environmental activism of the past, coupled with surfacing out of ongoing initiatives to control and protect forest by certain tribes in remote forest areas of Bihar, Orissa, and in sacred groves in North East became the premises to put forward the theory of co-management of forests. A successful example of involvement of communities for protection of an experimental forest plot in lieu of some benefits, in Midnapore, West Bengal in 1972 became the prototype to push forward the idea. In June 1991, the first resolution by the government of India written to Forest Secretaries of all the States and the union territories set the agenda to evolve mechanisms for involvement of communities and voluntary agencies for regeneration of degraded forest land. The various State government followed it by passing their respective State resolutions on JFM. So far 23 states have passed enabling orders for implementation of JFM. It emerged as an approach to forest regeneration and management under which the FD and the village community enter into an agreement to jointly protect and manage a particular patch of forest. In turn, the FD agrees to provide access to specified forest products to the members of village institution formed for the purpose.

The general model adopted for JFM by most of the states, specifies the need for the formation of a Village Forest Committee (VFC) and the organizational structure, membership norms & practices to be followed by the village institutions for the protection of a designated forest area. An executive body is formed out of the VFC. The membership criteria for executive committee as well as for VFC vary from state to state. An agreement is signed between the Forest Department and the VFC. The roles and responsibilities of both the forest department as well as the VFC are clarified in the various state government orders . The government orders also specify the sharing mechanism for timber and nontimber forest produce between the forest department and the VFC.

Various independent studies as well as the report of FSI 1999 indicate that the health of the forests improved after the implementation of JFM. Numerous studies have indicated ecological and economic benefits of JFM at the local level. (Khare et al, 2000). Over the last decade, the implementation of JFM threw up many issues and contradictions. Some of these were addressed, but some are still unresolved. Some of the issues are:

- **Notion of Community and Village Institutions**
  Community is not a homogenous entity . It is divided on caste, class, occupation and gender basis. Many of the state orders initially restricted the membership to one member of the household, which resulted in the formation of male dominated FPC thereby excluding

the women by default. Similarly, some of the states even did not consider stipulation of women's presence by design in the membership of the executive body. The very crucial issue raised by many active groups of practitioners and researchers was regarding the membership criteria in general body or the Forest Protection Committees. Many studies and experience-sharing platforms highlighted the need of institutional arrangement to make the participation of marginalized women and men mandatory in the decision-making process in the Village Institutions. This debate had a substantial effect in terms of policy-making. Many state orders, which considered one representative/household, subsequently amended their state orders in favour of Joint membership. The initial Madhya Pradesh Government order (10.12.91) considered one representative per household, while the second amended order (4.01.95) corrected the anomaly by introducing the provision for one male and one female per household to be the member of the VFC. The third revised resolution (7.02.2000) for the same state has further reserved 33 percent seats of the Executive Committee for women. The whole issue of institutionalized separate identity for women has further got impetus with the recent guidelines dated 21st February, 2000 issued by MoEF in this regard. The guidelines suggest that for ensuring meaningful participation of Women in JFM (i) *At least 50% members of the JFM general body should be women. For the general body meeting, the presence of at least 50% women members should be a prerequisite for holding the general body meeting. (ii) At least 33% of the membership in the JFM Executive Committee/ Management Committee should be filled from amongst the women members. The quorum for holding meetings of such Executive / Management Committee should be one-third of women executive members or a minimum of one whichever is more. One of the posts of office bearer i.e. president/ Vice-President / Secretary should be filled by a woman member of the Committee.* Another aspect which has considerable bearing on the success of JFM vis-a-vis participation of community is the prioritization of the management objective.

The State government since the colonial times, managed the forest for revenue from timber. The poor people in a village community are interested in managing the forest for fuelwood, fodder and other nontimber forest produce to meet the immediate basic needs. In the new system of Joint Forest Management, Forest Department showed the gold carrot in the form of a share of sale of timber in the distant future to the village community. This raised the conflict between the marginalized women and men dependent on forest and well-to-do families within the same community. In many villages in Gujarat, West Bengal, Bihar and Orissa, when protection began, women were barred from any form of collection, even of dry twigs. In some protected sites in Gujarat in 1993 and West Bengal in 1994, it was found that women who hitherto would spend one to two hours for a headload of firewood now spend four to five hours, and a journey of half a kilometer has in some cases lengthened to eight to nine kilometers (Aggarwal, 1997). It is for this reason that the orientation of management objectives for taking care of day-to-day needs of the people require interventions in terms of reworking of working plans as well as suitable silvicultural options for sustenance of multi-forest produce.

- **JFM ambit**: The initial June 1990 circular restricted the JFM to the *degraded forest areas*. Different states interpreted the term 'degraded forest' in different ways, which raised lots of confusion and placed the power of discretion with the forest department. Considerable lobbying by the supporters of JFM has been done in last decade to bring good and natural forest under the ambit of JFM. As a result, the recent guidelines of Feb 2000 from MoEF directed all the State government for coverage of JFM in good forest areas also. The protected area network has been still kept out of the realm of JFM, and many cases have also occurred where a forest area under JFM implementation is being converted into protected area .
- **Imbalance in power**: JFM as a concept has generated notions of equality of partners that is forest department and the village institution. In reality, instead of decentralization and nurturing of self governed and strong village institutions, forest bureaucracy has tried to exercise and retain its control by maneuvering the village institutions by its virtual control on the destiny of these institutions. In most of the orders, the village body has to be accountable to the forester incharge (Ranger/DFO), who has the unilateral power to disqualify the village institution. Only in very few places, village Institutions have been able to break the hegemony of the forest department, whereas in most of the external aided projects (World Bank funded M.P and A.P, DFID funded H.P and Uttaranchal forestry projects), though the projects have been structured for bringing transparency in the system and power redistribution, the FD had retained its strength and control by virtue of being the provider of incentives and employment under the project. The

unequal relationship leaves very negligible scope for the community to break the phenomena of corruption, *begari,* and oppression of village community at all levels, which has been prevalent throughout, with or without JFM. But at the same time, the health of the forests has improved, village funds have been created, though for most of the forest dependent communities, the phenomena of JFM has been like *nectar in the sieve*.

- **Livelihood versus JFM**: Another issue linked to people's participation for sustainable use of forests, is the question of food security. During the lean season, in the absence of other available livelihood opportunities for tribal and other marginalized women, they are being forced to cut fuelwood from forests to meet the cash needs. This may result in over-exploitation of forests. In the absence of conducive environment for livelihood opportunities, expecting people to participate in the protection of the forest is not a practical approach. Moreover, headloading of fuelwood for sale reflects the abject poverty conditions. Here, headloading is nothing but a forced wastage of human resource. Exploitation of forest can only be overcome in these regions by providing alternative employment and opportunities to people, which require comprehensive regional planning and political will, rather than a sectoral approach.

There have been many more issues in the implementation of JFM at the regional and the national levels than mentioned above. The implementation of JFM has also witnessed that the policy and theoretical constructs are moving much ahead of the actual practice in field.

Findings

The decade long experience with JFM shows that it has certainly tried to shift the people-forest department relation in a desirable direction at least conceptually. It has been able to bring relative transparency in government working and has awakened the desire for it to be more. It has also given the legitimacy and moral grounds to the village community in accessing forest, has sought expertise and trained probing lens of professionals and Voluntary agencies from other fields in the closed fort of forestry, and above all succeeded in regenerating forests. In response to the forest bureaucracy's inherent attempt to turn any concept of power-sharing into a project to run its own system, attempts are being made to bring in the concept of **community forestry** over to the system of Joint Forest Management, where the communities will become legally registered bodies to get any kind of financial support and forest department role would be limited to the technical support only. There is need to link the learnings emanating from the forestry sector with the development sector in general, since the progression of JFM in search of empowerment of rural community and good governance in forest department has the potential to inform the other parallel processes ongoing in agriculture, irrigation and other sectors as well.

References

Agarwal, B. (1997), *Environment Action, Gender Equity and Women's Participation in Development and Change* (Vol. 23), Institute of Social Studies, Delhi.

Khare, *et al.*, (2000). JFM in Practice: Dilemmas and Prospects in Mayers and Morrison (eds) *Joint Forest Management Policy, Practice and Prospects*, 2nd edition: London.

Poffenberger, M. (1995), *Public Lands Reform: India's Experiences with Joint Forest Management.*

National Forestry Action Programme

6

M. Satyanarayana

The International Setting

The Forestry and Environment have assumed significance after the Rio Earth Summit in 1992. The United Nations Conference for Environment & Development (UNCED), the Commission on sustainable Development (CSD) and the Inter-governmental Panel on Forestry (IPF) have recognized the need for rehabilitation and sustainable management of Tropical Forest resources and recommended to launch strategies to arrest de-forestation and halt degradation. Consequently, the Tropical Forest Action Plan (TFAP) was launched in 1985 with the following aims:

- To increase awareness of the problem of deforestation and to mobilize all levels of society to address it.
- To introduce Inter-sectoral planning approaches, involving all relevant stakeholders in order to allow formulation of more effective policies and programmes.

- To mobilize national and international resources to assist preparation and implementation of National Forest Programmes (NFAPs) in a coordinated manner.

TFAP was adopted by the World Forestry congress in Mexico in July, 1985. In the Hague meeting held in Nov, 1985, representatives of bilateral and multilateral development aid organizations, supported by International NGOs, confirmed the acceptance of TFAP as a framework to guide their bilateral and multilateral cooperation activities for sustainable management of tropical forests. Further more, they accepted the need for translating the global TFAP into National TFAPs consistent with the national priorities and development plans. It was also agreed to review the strategies for forestry development and to identify the priorities of the actions for formulating NFAPs.

The Indian Context

The NFAP is designed to identify the issues and to address the programmes to be implemented for achieving sustainable forestry development in India by harmonizing the activities of all stakeholders. The formulation of NFAP was undertaken by the Government of India with financial assistance from United Nations Development Programme (UNDP) and technical support from the Food and Agriculture Organisation (FAO). The Project was initiated in 1993 and completed in June 1999.

The process involved coordinated Center-State strategic planning to promote and implement sustainable forest resources conservation, management and development, with well-defined inter-sectoral linkages that blend with the National Development Plans. A considerable amount of information was generated during the NFAP preparation process. Initially, documents included 24 State forest section reviews, 16 special topic reports, 5 reports by international consultants, 5 regional synthesis reports and a three-volume draft forest sector review. After the preparation of these papers, the Ministry of Environment and Forests organized a two-day National Workshop in New Delhi in March, 1995, followed by 5 Regional Workshops during June-August 1995. These meetings considered the scope and content of State Forest Action Programmes (SFAPs) and the State governments were asked to formulate SFAPs which were later compiled into a Three-Volume NFAP report (Vol.1: Background Information and Situation Analysis; Vol. II: Policy and Institutional Reforms, issues, Strategies and Implementation mechanisms; and Vol. III: Investment Proposals).

This National Forestry Action Programme is a comprehensive Long-Term strategic plan for the next twenty years to achieve the goal of sustainable development of forests and also to increase the forest/tree cover in the country to the desired 33 per cent of the geographical area i.e. 1/3rd area of the country. This document is a compilation of the State Forest Action Programmes prepared by the States and also incorporates the recommendations of the Regional and National Workshop on NFAP. This document does not summarise the contents or reconcile differences in the various reports, but instead analyses and highlights major issues to facilitate urgent and meaningful action and decision-making.

It takes into account the basic objectives of National forestry Policy, 1988 which envisages the following:

- Conserving the natural heritage;
- Increasing substantially the forest/tree cover through massive afforestation and social forestry programmes;
- Meeting the requirements of fuel wood, fodder, minor forest produce and small timber of the rural and tribal populations,
- Increasing the productivity of forests.
- Encouraging efficient utilization of forest produce;
- Creating a massive people's movement.
- Maintenance of environmental stability.

The forests play an important role in day-to-day life of every Indian, specially those who are living in and around forests. They also help in environmental sustainability and support development of food production. They generate employment for the tribals and rural poor and can play a pivotal role in the rural poverty alleviation programmes. India is having 2.5 per cent of World's geographical area and only 1.8 per cent of World's forests while supporting 17% of Planet's human population and 18% of livestock population. The present document aims at sustainable development of 76.5 million ha. of forests which includes enriching tree cover over 31 million ha. of forest land and bringing over 29 million ha. non-forest area under tree cover through agro-forestry, farm forestry, urban forestry etc.

Programme Components

The main components of the programme are:

(I) Protection of Existing Forest Resources:

It has three main-sub programmes of (i) forest protection, (ii) soil and water conservation, and (iii) protected areas and biodiversity conservation. These include the works of forest survey, demarcation and mapping, protection of forest boundary, inventory of forest resources, prevention of illicit activities like thefts, pilferage and encroachment, control of deforestation, establishing system of legal deterrents, biodiversity conservation, protected area management, rationalization of shifting cultivation, settlement of tenurial issues, preventing conversion of forests for non-forest use, protection of forests from grazing, pests and diseases, protection against poaching, and fire, control of desertification, watershed protection, protection of fragile ecosystems including mangroves, development of conservation strategy, ex situ and in situ conservation of genetic resources, joint forest management, eco-development, ecotourism, introduction of appropriate incentives, strengthening working plan and other related issues.

(II) Improvement of Forest Productivity :

It has four main sub-programmes of (i) rehabilitation of degraded forest, (ii) research and technology development, (iii) development of Non Wood Forest Products (NWFPs) and (iv) assisting private initiatives with community participation. These involve mainly research, improvement in technology, enrichment planting, soil and water conservation, regeneration, rehabilitation and afforestation, bioprospecting, promoting better growth and yield through better management, integrated management for wood and NWFPs, other forms of multiple use management, increased use of lesser known and secondary species, improving density of stocking, valuation of forest-derived services, and non-use values, domestication of species both flora and fauna, research on short rotation, high-yielding and genetically improved varieties for plantations, provenance trials, nursery technology improvement, mixed cropping and multiple cropping, fuelwood and pasture development, establishment of GIS etc.

(III) Reduction of Total Demand:

It has three main sub-programmes for the efficient uses of (i) fuel wood and fodder, (ii) timber and (iii) NWFPs. This includes the programmes for reduction of demand placed on forests through the technology of preservation, seasoning, substitutions and other measures for the efficient utilization of forest products and also through extensive biomass plantations, works of improved, waster-free and low-impact harvesting of forest products, pre-harvest and post-harvest operations, improvement of processing technology providing high conversion factor and reduced wastage, chemical treatments, improved chullas, improved cooking practices and alternative fuels, rotational grazing and stall feeding, value-added downstream processing to divert labour from primary processing, quality control, promote substitution of solid wood, reducing demand through market manipulation and pricing mechanism etc.

(IV) Strengthening of Policy and Institutional Framework:

It has three main sub-programmes i.e. strengthening of (i) central forestry administration, (ii) central forestry institutions, and (iii) State forestry administration and institutions. These include the development of infrastructure like buildings, communications, etc., and strengthening of staff including HRD. This issue also covered all aspects of capacity building, forest policy and legislation, public forest administration and organizational structure, research, planning and budgeting, rationalizing the revenue system, safeguarding intellectual property rights relating to forestry, restructuring of sectoral institutions, sectoral and project planning, development of data systems, investment analysis, monitoring and evaluation, extension and public education, dissemination of information etc.

(V) Expansion of forest area:

It has two main sub-programmes (i) tree plantation on forest and non-forest lands, and (ii) people's participation in plantations and its protection. It includes the programmes of creation of plantation forests through wasteland reclamation, afforestation and promotion of agro-forestry, desert reclamation, strip plantations along roads, railway lines, canals, farm forestry, urban forestry, shelterbelts, industrial plantations, greening and landscaping.

Resource Constraints

The programme will be implemented by the States/ UTs. The implementation of NFAP requires huge financial resources and the total investment estimate for the State sector is Rs. 1232321 millions and for the Central sector is Rs. 106706 millions. Total requirement for the country is Rs. 1339 billions (US$32 billion) over the next twenty years.

The availability of internal resources to this vital sector is inadequate. This Ministry has already organized the First Conference of International Donor Agencies jointly with FAO and the UNDP on 27th Septemeber, 1999 in New Delhi. Efforts are being made to mobilize resources both from external and internal sources to increase allocation to the Forestry Sector in the coming years for implementation of the NFAP to achieve the desired objective of the sustainable development of forests and environmental security of the future generations.

References:

Government of India, Ministry of Environment and Forests, *National Forestry Action Programme*, Volumes I & II, New Delhi, 1999.

Joint Forest Management:
Indian and Canadian Experiences

7

K.R.G. Nair*

Introduction

The past few decades have witnessed considerable emphasis on the sustainability of development. An important constituent of this is related to forests and the issue here seems to be a very simple one of ensuring that the % forest area is kept at a certain minimum level so that there can be continued commercial exploitation of the forest resources for the benefit of mankind over generations. But this is far from the truth

* The author wishes to thank Mr. Satyanarayana of the Department of Forests of the Ministry of Environment of the Government of India, Dr. Nadini Sundar of the Institute of Economic Growth, Dr. Jean Manore of Trent University, the Librarian of the Shastri Indo-Canadian Institute and researchers at the Society for Promotion of Wastelands development and World Wide Fund for Nature – India for material, data and discussions at various stages during the preparation of this paper. The usual disclaimers apply and the responsibility for any errors or inconsistencies is entirely the author's.

because of the conflicting interest-groups or stake-holders involved and the multiplicity of objectives in formulating policy.

For example, in the case of India, the proponents of scientific forestry - the foresters - blame the forest people for unsustainable forest development in India. This is explicitly brought out in the Forest Survey of India, 1998 which categorically states that "excessive grazing and over-dependence on firewood for domestic energy are the two factors most responsible for depletion of forests in the country." The National Commission on Agriculture of the Government of India in its report is even more outright in its condemnation of the forest people. It specifically mentions that "Free supply of forest produce to the rural population and their rights and privileges have brought destruction to the forests". The clear policy implication that the foresters derive is that the population of forest people should be controlled and excluded from forests in the interests of regeneration and hence of sustainable development of forests.

Diametrically opposite is the view held by Non-government organizations (NGO's) and academics. According to them, only the forest people know how to preserve the forests. They stress the historical fact that this was being successfully done till the 19th century till which time there was no degradation of forests. They highlight the fact such degradation began only after the British came to India. They blame the collusion between foresters and forest-based industries for the degradation of forests in India. According to them, this collusion has led to extraction of more timber than the forest can bear, clear-cutting of natural forests for plantations and also to conversion of mixed forests to mono-culture, wringing havoc to forests in India.

As regards the multiplicity of objectives, the listing in this regard done in the National Forest Policy Resolution of the Government of India in 1988 speaks for itself. It mentions four groups of objectives. Firstly there are environmental objectives including maintenance of environmental stability and conserving bio-diversity. Then there are livelihood objectives like the provision of tribal and other groups with firewood, fodder, minor forest produce and construction timber. Thirdly there is the national objective of maintaining one-third of the country's area and two-third of hill and mountainous areas under forest cover. There is also mention of the social objective of creation of people's movement involving women in forest areas. In view of these different objectives, it is quite clear that there is no single maximand in this regard and one has to work out a composite objective function.

We live in the age of liberalization and decentralized planning and management. The claims of the different stake-holders have, therefore, to be given due weightage. But this has to be done in such a way that the multiplicity of objectives are met to the maximum possible extent. It would hence be interesting to examine the way in which forest-related issues are tackled in two large democratic federations of the world – India and Canada. There are, of course, considerable diversities within each of these countries in this regard. This paper contains the results of a preliminary study in this direction and is hence confined to a comparison in this regard between Dalki in the state of Orissa in India and Temagami in the province of Ontario in Canada. It is split into three parts. Part one contains a study of Dalki forests. Part two contains a study of the Temagami experience in this regard. Part three compares the two sets of experiences to draw meaningful inferences in this regard.

Forest Management in Dalki

Orissa is one of the least developed states of India. This is true irrespective of whether we consider economic or social indicators of development. Among the fifteen major Indian states, Orissa ranks the second from below in terms of per capita state domestic product and of per cent people above the poverty line. The state has the highest infant mortality rate and the second lowest expectation of life at birth.

Sambalpur district is on the northwestern edge of the state and Dalki forest is in Lapanga village of this district.

The Dalki forest – named after a goddess who will eat away anyone who will enter the forest with destruction in mind – consists mainly of wasteland. It is managed by a village forest protection committee which dates back to around a hundred years. As pointed out by many including Nandini Sundar (1996), the Dalki forest has witnessed successful forest protection as a result of community management. Certain areas have been demarcated for cutting every 2-3 years in selective rotational cutting. As a result, the average height of sal trees in Dalki forest is 35-40 metres. The forest protection committee of the village has actually received a number of awards for its efficient functioning and these include the Surakya award in 1976 and the Prakriti Mitra award in 1985-86.

The basic question however is whether the forest management practices adopted in Dalki cater to the subsistence needs of all the villagers. Out of the 358 households, 43.3% are of landless labor, 41.9% are of small and marginal farmers and only 1.67% are of large farmers. The first two categories of households and particularly the first category is very much dependent on the collection and sale of non-timber forest produce (NTFP) like Tendu and Sal leaves out of which leaf plates are made. But, as pointed out Nandini Sundar (2001) and Dhanagare (2000), just as in the other parts of India, the focus of joint forest management in Dalki also seems to be on timber production and adequate attention is not paid to the livelihood needs of the forest people for NTFP. For instance, in Dalki the committee does not allow any pruning of tendu bushes in the forest, which means that they do not generate new leaves.

There are also serious doubts as to whether the system being evolved is democratic and equitable. The residents are classified as praja A consisting of landlords whose ancestors were involved in forest protection efforts, Praja B consisting of other landlords and sukhvasis or landless residents. Only a praja can be a member of the executive body of the committee. There is also price discrimination for products on the basis of this classification. Praja A households are entitled to timber at the lowest rate while the others have to pay 1.5 times the praja A rate.

The net result of all this is that while there is considerable protection of forests in Lapanga, much of it is at the cost of the neighboring Moulabhanga reserve forest, to which the landless from Lapanga hop across to meet their subsistence needs.

The Temagami Experience

The Temagami region is located in the north-eastern part of the province of Ontario, the largest province of Canada in terms of population and also one of the richest in terms of per capita domestic product. The exotic name Temagami is derived from Teme-Auguming meaning the place of the deep water. It covers N'Daki Menan – the homeland or the ancestral hunting territory of Teme-Augeming-Anishnabai – the people of the deep water. The Ministry of Natural Resources of Ontario has a district known as Temagami including Lake Temagami, village Temagami and Lady Evelyn lake. There used to be also a forest area named Temagami. From the 1st of January 1998, there is also a town there with the name Temagami with a municipality. But as pointed out by many including Hodgins and Benedickson (1989), the precise and constant definition of the area is a difficult and elusive exercise and will hence not be attempted in this paper.

It is universally accepted that the Temagami area is one of the few remaining accessible regions where the age-old beauty of the Canadian north can be witnessed and experienced. It has long been a recreational area. With more than 2400 kilometers of inter-connected lakes, rivers and portages, it provides a canoe route network more extensive than in any other provincial park in Canada. The oldest canoe-tripping camp-Keewaydeen-has been active in Temagami since 1983 and is located in Lake Temagami. There is also abundance of fish and wild life, remnant old growth forest stands, potential mineral deposits and significant cultural heritage routes and sites. The rugged topography also provides for excellent hiking and people can travel thousands of kilometers by snowmobile in the region.

A historical perspective on the Temagami region has been very vividly brought out in a document prepared by Northwatch et. al. (1996). According to the document

"For thousands of years, rocky escarpments, forested valleys and fish-rich lakes of Temagami have evolved according to the forces of wind, water and sun. Plants, animals and humans have all lived in a stable ecological framework that changed slowly and provided life for all. Since the late 19th century, human uses have begun to test the resilience and capacity of Temagami lands and waters as well as the entire ecological region. European settlement, followed by extensive and intensive trapping, logging, fire control, dam building and mining have altered the face of the region more than any other event or influence since glaciation...

The changes to the ecology of the land have caused increasing conflict for its human inhabitants. None more so than those who were here first and who were most dependent on land in its original untrammeled form. In a land they called N'Daki Menan, the Teme – Augama – Anishnabai had lived a semi-nomadic existence of hunting and gathering for 1000s of years and developed one of the largest inter-connected canoe route systems in North America. By the 1930's the political demands created by logging, mining and tourism had forced them on to a one square mile island and deprived them of their way of life.

Later Europeans began to see and experience the results of the activities brought by settlers to Temagami. The often conflicting land uses for recreation, tourism, logging and mining became more and more difficult to reconcile and the resources on which they were based eroded, while demand continued to grow".

Thus, over time Temagami has become in fact, almost synonymous with the debate over resource extraction methods, native land rights and also wilderness protection. By the mid-80's most of the environmental issues that emerged in Ontario actually centered around Temagami which was hence looked upon by many as a microcosm for such matters. Recreationists and environmentalists were looking for more protection of wilderness values and of road-less area. As early as in the 1970's aboriginal concerns for land and discontent over the crown's refusal to acknowledge aboriginal rights had reached new heights with a land caution being filed in 1973 by the Bear Island foundation. While anglers and hunters clamored for public use of access roads to interior areas, environmentalists opposed this idea as well as the pressure for more logging. There was pressure from the commercial foresters and mining for greater exploitation and use of these natural resources whereas those with general concern for sustainability of the natural resource base expressed serious reservations about steps in this direction. Conflicts over native land rights, industrial forest use and wilderness protection became almost daily occurrences. Matters came to such a head that in 1987-88, there was a massive public outcry and even displays of civil disobedience.

Many including Hodgins and Benedickson (1989) attribute the flashpoint in the mid-80's to lack of a concerted and proper forest policy in Temagami. It is true that early in the 20th century, the Ontario government designated Temagami, regarded as primary pineland, as a forest reserve with the stated intention that sustained yield forest management might be implemented there under the guidance of professional foresters. The policy could however not be successfully followed because of many reasons. There was no continuous supervision and monitoring to see that the declared goal is attained. There was, in fact, no sustained intervention in planning and harvesting techniques to ensure sustained yield pine forestry. It has been pointed out by some that the Minsitry of Natural Resources under-estimated the age at which pine became overmature and was unduly optimistic about natural regeneration without fire. There was also accusations that the Ministry of Natural Resources was determining the size of the allowable cut to suit the needs of local industry rather than considering the ecological reality. Another equally damaging account of forest policy was by Baskerville (1986) that was highly critical of the way non-timber forest produce was neglected in the policy. Further, while there was an initial outburst of successful implementation and attempts were made to control forest fires, alternate land uses inconsistent with the declared goal could not be controlled. This is mainly attributable to the fact that all aspects of the issue were not considered in formulating policy nor were all stake-holders involved in decision-making. The net result was that sustained development in forest reserves did not become a public objective sustained by political will.

More rational and concerted attempts are being made towards more coordinated, meaningful and participatory forest management in Temagami since early 90's. The residents of Temagami and of the islands of the unorganized areas of Temagami worked together on a joint planning board to work and land use matters. In April 1996, the Temagami Joint Planning council submitted its final report to the Ministry of Natural Resources with two sets of recommendations. One set related to recreation, cultural heritage, fisheries, fire, landscape ecology, minerals, provincial parks, tourism, timber and wildlife values. Another addressed problems of governance, interests of and need to involve the area's aboriginal peoples, future resource management and education. In June 1996, the Ministry of Natural Resources approved most of the recommendations without any change and some, after slight modifications. This concerted and participatory approach is bound to bring about qualitative changes in forest and overall resource management in Temagami.

Inferences

We can draw certain broad inferences form this comparative analysis of forest management in India and in Canada. It is clear from the study here that the issue is not a simple one. The objective of forest management cannot be just sustained yield of timber. The importance of non-timber forest produce particularly for the livelihood of forest people should not be ignored. It has further to be borne in mind that sustainability of forests cannot just mean sustaining, by scientific forest management, commercial exploitation of forests. There are a multiplicity of objectives and often conflicting interest-groups or stake-holders. Solutions do not seem to, lay in simple orders to be passed and implemented by government departments without public support. In getting community participation, it is necessary that all affected parties, including the original inhabitants, should have their voices heard.

It is true that this preliminary analysis is confined to chosen portions of India and of Canada. Orissa has a longer history of active forest protection groups than most other states of India and has also a large number of NGOs involved in this work. It is the first among the Indian states to pass a resolution to bring about Joint Forest Management and this was done much before the government of India passed such a resolution in the year 1990. Therefore, while it is true, as is shown by Nandini Sundar (2001), Dhanagare (2000) and Khare et al. (2000) that general inferences in this regard are likely to be similar irrespective of the state considered. If we are to work out more detailed inferences for the whole of India, experiences in this regard, which are likely to be different in the case of other states have also to be studied. As regards Canada there is all the more reason to do so because many including Jean Manore (2000) feel after a comparative analysis of participatory forest management in the different provinces of Canada that some other provinces like Manitoba may be better instances of model participatory forest management than Temagami. Meaningful and detailed inferences can hence be drawn only on the basis of an in-depth comparative study of inter-regional experiences in participatory forest management in India and in Canada.

Reference

Baskerville, Gordon.L, (1986), *"An Audit of Management of the Crown Forests of Ontario"*, Report to the Ontario Ministry of Natural Resources, Toronto, August

Dhangare, D.N. (2000), Joint Forest Management in U.P. People. Panchayats and Women, *Economic and Political Weekly,* Vol. 35, No. 37, September 9, pp.3315-3324.

Hodgins, Bruce W, and James Benedickson (1989), *The Temagami Experience*, The University of Toronto Press, Toronto

Jean Manore (2000), *Private Communication to the Author*

Khare, A, *et.al.* (2000), *Joint Forest Management*, Policy Practice and Prospects, Policy That Works For People Series no. 3, World Wild Life Fund for Nature India, New Delhi and International Institute for Environment and Development, London.

Nandini Sundar, Abha Mishra and Neeraj Peter (1996), "Defending the Dalki Forest; 'Joint' Forest Management in Lapanga". *Economic and Political Weekly*, Vol 31, no 45-46, pp 3021-3025

Nandini Sundar (2001), *Branching Out: A Comparative Study of Joint Forest Management in Four States*, Oxford University Press, New Delhi.

Northwatch, B.L. *et.al.* (1996), *The New Temagami Forest Deciding on a Sustainable Future*, (mimeographed)

PART-III

Sectoral Aspects

Sustainable Development and the Indian Energy Sector

8

V. Raghuraman

Introduction

Energy is closely linked to economic development and environment quality. Significant growth in energy consumption in developing countries will be both essential and inevitable in the coming decades in order to support their economic development. But increased energy consumption will also lead to higher emissions of greenhouse gases(GHG). This should be taken as a matter of serious concern in order to make the growth path sustainable.

India, like many other developing countries, has been experiencing a high pace of industrialization. The **industrial sector** in India is a major energy user, accounting for about 52 per cent of the commercial energy consumption. **Per capita consumption** of primary energy in India is only 277 Kg of oil equivalent (koe) which is just 3.5 per cent of USA, 6.8 per cent of Japan, 37 per cent of Asia and 18.7 per cent of world average. Although India is rich in coal and abundantly endowed with renewable energy resources in the form of solar, wind, hydel and bio-energy, its hydrocarbon reserve is really very small. India is a net importer of energy whose major energy need is being met through imports mainly in the form of crude oil and petroleum products. The huge energy import bill is largely responsible for energy supply shortages, which have led to energy insecurity. The sub-optimal consumption of the commercial energy adversely affects the productive sectors, which in turn hampers economic growth.

Energy GDP de-coupling:

In industrialized countries, since the oil shocks of the 1970's, we have seen that growth of GDP has been realized without a corresponding growth of energy demand. A de-coupling has taken place. One can explain this energy GDP de-coupling in the following manner. In the developed countries, there has been a shift from energy-intensive industrial sectors to less energy-intensive service sectors. Moreover, in certain end use sectors such as households, personal disposable income has reached such a level, at which energy consumption of energy-intensive appliances have attained a saturation level. Finally, technological progress has increased energy efficiency, keeping the demand stable without constraining the growth of economic activity. As a result of these factors, carbon emissions in some OECD countries have been stable or declined over the years. In a developing country like India, where energy consumption is so low, such a state of de-coupling is far way to reach. In India, it has been found empirically that energy consumption causes economic growth without any feedback effect (Adjaye, 2000; Masih & Masih, 1996). So, proper policy framework should be undertaken in the energy sector, in terms of more investment, improved efficiency of use, diversification of energy supplies and cost-effectiveness of resource utilization for sustainable growth.

Energy Intensity:

Historical data on energy-intensity for some of the developed countries (e.g. Germany, France, UK, USA etc.)

revealed that initially, these countries' energy-intensity had increased because of the development of heavy industries and infrastructure, then peaked and finally began to decline due to

- shifting from non-commercial to commercial energy;
- more efficient use of commercial energy and
- substituting fossil fuels by electricity in many cases.

In most of the developing countries, energy intensity has been increasing as expected, since they have embarked on the path of growth and relied heavily on the development of infrastructure and heavy industries. Unfortunately, **energy-intensity** in India is one of the highest in comparison to other developed and developing countries. For example, it is 3.7 times of Japan, 1.55 times of USA, 1.47 times of Asia and 1.5 times of world average. Thus, there is a huge scope for energy conservation and efficiency improvement programs in the country.

Energy-Efficiency:

Energy-efficiency involves efficient utilization of resources, which is a key to sustainable development. It is a measure of productivity provided per unit of energy consumed. Improving energy-efficiency increases productivity, significantly reduces the GHG emissions, reduces solid waste production and thermal pollution.

Policies and programs that have been used in countries worldwide to improve efficiency in the energy sector can be classified as

- Good house-keeping practices
- Regulation and/or Standards
- Industrial cogeneration
- Fuel switching
- Fiscal policies like taxes, tax rebates, subsidies etc.

- Agreement/Targets
- Benchmarking
- Energy audits
- Information dissemination and demonstration and
- Research and development.

The industrial sector in India, inspite of a *Win-Win* situation, did not pay much attention to energy-efficiency improvement program due to three main reasons:

- Most of the manufacturing units still depend on old machinery
- Relatively high cost of capital as compared to European/USA standards.
- Uncertainty about the long-term growth of the particular industrial sector.

A recent World Bank report shows that Indian Industry has the potential to save 20 to 30 per cent of total energy consumption. Table 1 indicates the average energy conservation potential in various sectors and in various energy-intensive industries.

Efficiency improvement in the Indian power sector requires special attention since the sector has been suffering from chronic supply shortage, lack of capital investment for new capacity addition and environmental problems associated with coal-based power plants. High auxiliary consumption and T&D (Transmission & Distribution) losses further aggravate the situation.

Macroeconomic policies sometimes discourage to undertake energy-efficiency measures. Environmentally harmful subsidies reduce the private costs of producers and consumers resulting in over-utilization of the scarce resources. Energy subsidies in India, for example, lead to energy-intensive economic structures and technologies, and wasteful management practices.

According to a World Resources Institute (WRI) study, by late 90's, bilateral banks made up largely of Export Credit

Agencies (ECAs) accounted for 31% of all long-term financing received by developing countries. ECAs appear to be investing heavily in the long-term consumption, rather than reducing the developing countries' dependence of fossil fuels, and hence ultimately the associated GHG emissions. The reasons could be

- no credible environmental guidelines
- no transparency regarding information sharing
- in most industrialized countries, trade and finance ministries are set apart from the environmental ministry and thus there is a lack of policy coherence.

Energy and Environment:

In India, the major source of primary energy is coming from coal and it is expected that coal will continue its share in the future. But burning of coal creates a host of serious environmental problems requiring emission control and waste disposal. Coal has the highest CO_2 emission coefficient with respect to oil and gas. Inspite of the fact that India emits only 0.2 tons per capita of carbon dioxide from fossil fuels (compared to 5.2 tons for the US and a world average of 1.2 tons), it is now the world's sixth largest carbon dioxide emitter. Another alarming fact is that India might be the world's most populated country by 2025.

Thus, a high population growth, predominance of coal in energy generation, low energy efficiency and a high economic growth path because of the low-income level is causing concern in the international circles about India's future GHG emission.

Sustainability and Kyoto Protocol:

The emission of CO_2, the leading global warming gas, has increased 12-fold during the 20th Century. It is estimated that the present concentration of CO_2 in the atmosphere is 30 per cent more than when extensive burning of CO_2 began during the Industrial Revolution.

The impacts of global warming are being felt on almost all the countries in the form of increase in extreme events like floods, draughts, cyclones, spread of infectious diseases etc. There is worse to come, unless necessary steps are taken to reduce the rising trend of CO_2 emission. In 1992, the United Nation Framework Convention on Climate Change (UNFCCC) was adopted to stabilize the concentration of GHG in the atmosphere to a level that would avoid "dangerous anthropogenic interference" with the earth's climate system. The UNFCCC includes voluntary commitments for most industrialized countries to reduce their GHG emissions to 1990 levels by the year 2000. Developing countries didn't have any commitments under UNFCCC. Kyoto Protocol was adopted in December 1997 and if ratified, it will bind developed countries to achieve the agreed level of emission reductions by 2008-2012. The protocol includes three mechanisms to enable flexible implementation of the treaty: Emission Trading (ET), the Clean Development Mechanism (CDM) and Joint Implementation (JI). Such "flexible mechanisms" are designed to be mutually beneficial to both the developed and developing countries. Investors from developed countries (also referred to as Annex B countries) could fund projects that reduce GHG emission in a developing country. Developed countries achieve emission reduction compliance at lower cost while capital-starved developing countries benefit by achieving much-desired sustainable development path by getting access to finances and the state-of- the-art technology. The emission reductions in the developing countries can be achieved in the following areas:

Energy

- Improved end-use efficiencies in industries, services and households;
- Efficient transmission and distribution systems;
- Fuel switching;
- Renewable energy technologies;
- Clean conversion technologies for conventional fuels.

Agriculture

- Fertilizer control schemes;
- Introduction of crops with greater carbon sequestration capacity;
- Livestock management, manure treatment and feeding.

Forestry

- Afforestation and reforestation programs;
- Increasing forests' carbon sequestration capability;
- Reçycling or permanent storage of carbon in harvested biomass.

Transportation

- Improved vehicle efficiency;
- Fuel systems with lower emissions;
- Modal shifts;
- Transport demand management;
- Improved infrastructure.

Waste Management

- Gas recovery from landfills;
- Biogas plants;
- Recycling;
- Composting.

Industry

- Paper industry;
- Cement industry;
- Aluminum production.

Table 1 summarizes the results of a study of some energy-intensive sectors in India. It is evident that the investment projects could produce substantial reduction in GHG emissions.

Credit Rating Information Services of India Limited (CRISIL), using Top-Down Modeling Approach found that the CDM could account for between 397-503 Million Metric tons of Carbon (MMtC) emission reduction required of Annex B in 2010 or between 33%-55% of the total reductions required. The corresponding CDM flows could be between $5.2-$17.4 billion. Using marginal costs of abatement in different countries to estimate the flow of CDM funds, it is estimated that India would collect between 7%-12% of the total global market for CDM-led investment.

CRISIL pointed out the additional risks associated with CDM projects, which are:

- Uncertainty regarding the implementation of Kyoto protocol
- Risk of employing new and unproven technologies for emission reduction
- Returns not being commensurate with the underlying risk
- Uncertainty of valuation of CERs (**Certified Emission Reductions**) affecting the determination of project economics
- Risk of the project not being found CDM eligible after implementation, and
- In the absence of clear procedures, the transaction costs and implementation time could be high for initial CDM projects.

Conclusion

India ranks sixth in the world so far as the total energy consumption is concerned, but India still needs much more energy to keep pace with its development objectives. Energy scarcity is becoming a major barrier and could obstruct the stream of development in India. India needs proper initiatives to promote its energy portfolio diversification, integrated resource planning and energy conservation and efficiency improvement programs, which will not only meet the country's future energy demand for rapid economic growth, but also protect the environment in a sustainable manner.

India has a great potential to reduce its GHG emissions and "flexible mechanisms" can help a lot to achieve this. India could take the advantages of "flexible mechanisms", adoption of which could fetch the economy wide benefits by increasing the foreign direct investment, technology transfer and employment generation.

References

Adjaye A.J., (2000), The Relationship between Energy Consumption, Energy Prices and Economic Growth: Time Series Evidence from Asian Developing Countries. *Energy Economics* 22, pp 615-625.

Masih A.M.M. and Rumi Masih (1996), Energy Consumption, Real Income and Temporal Causality: Results from a Multi-country Study based on Cointegration and Error-Correction Modeling Techniques. *Energy Economics* 18, pp 165-183.

Raghuraman, V., (2000), Energy efficiency for green business. UNDP *Industry and Environment* 23 (3): pp 48-51.

Price, L., & E. Worrell (2000), *International Industrial Sector Energy Efficiency Policies*. Energy Analysis Department, Lawrence Berkeley National Laboratory.

Confederation of Indian Industries: Papers and Publications (*www.ciionline.org*)

World Resource Institute (WRI): Papers and Publications (*www.wri.org*)

Table 1: Energy Saving Potential

Sector/ Industry	Energy Saving Potential
Domestic & Commercial	20%
Transport	20%
Agriculture	30%
Industries	25%
Iron & Steel	10%
Fertilizers	15%
Textiles	25%
Cement	15%
Chlor-alkali	15%
Pulp & Paper	25%
Aluminium	10%
Ferrous Foundry	20%
Petrochemicals	15%
Glass & Ceramics	20%
Refineries	10%

(Source: CII Newsletter, Dec. 2000)

Policy and Institutional Issues in Grid Connected Wind Energy Development in India

9

Chintan Shah

Introduction

India is the world's fifth largest investor in wind power and the largest wind power producer in developing countries with 1267 MW of installed wind power capacity as on December, 2000.

The spurt in private sector participation in wind energy sector started in 1992, after the announcement of the "Private Power Policy" of 1991(CEA, 1991) and the availability of a range of incentives by the government.

After a period of explosive growth that made India the world's third largest (at, present fifth) producer of wind power, investment fell sharply from mid-1996, the possible reasons being as follows

- Lowering of tax-credit benefits due to levying of MAT (minimum alternate tax) and lowering of corporate income tax by the Union Government in 1995/96 and 1996/97 respectively, which reduced the attractiveness of wind as a tax-management option

- Withdrawal of third-party sale in some states
- Low CF (Capacity factor/plant load factor) achieved by wind turbines. (TERI, 1999)

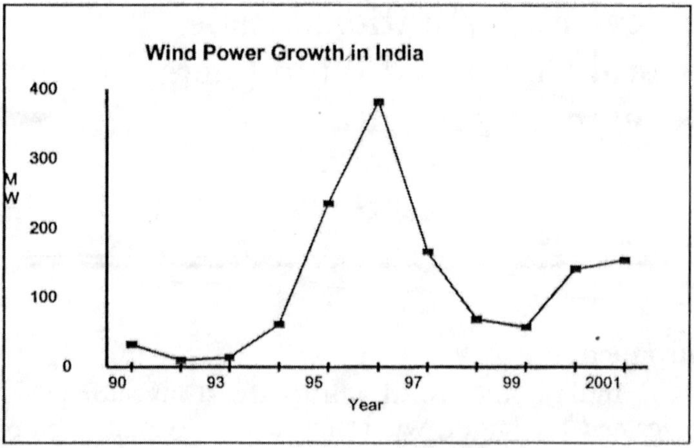

Some other indirect causes are as follows:

- Negligible foreign investments in Indian wind energy projects
- Higher interest rates

This paper tries to critically evaluate the factors responsible for wind power development, in order to provide lessons for policy-makers wishing to promote the successful development of wind power sector in India and other countries.

Wind energy programme in retrospect

The first systematic efforts to harness wind energy in the country were undertaken during the late fifties and early sixties by the Council of Scientific and Industrial Research (CSIR) at the National Aeronautical Laboratory (NAL), mainly in the area of water pumping windmills. However, owing to limited interest and relevance in the energy scene then, this work was closed down in 1966. The oil crisis of 1973 revived interest in the country, and in the National Science and Technology Plan specific recommendations were made on the harnessing of renewable sources of energy, including wind energy.

During the Sixth Five-Year Plan (1980-85) the focus was mainly on the development and demonstration of water pumping windmill technology. Renewable energy programme started in right earnest only with the establishment of the Department of non-conventional energy sources (DNES) in the Ministry of Power in 1982. Up to the mid-eighties, work in this area continued to be concentrated on water pumping and stand alone wind electric generators. A wind energy data handbook was published in 1983 based on an analysis of information and data on wind available from the vast network of meteorological observatories. This served as a preliminary data source for the early initiatives in India during the Seventh Five-Year Plan (1985-90). Later, an extensive wind resource programme (MNES, 1995/1996) was initiated through the Field Research Unit (FRU), Bangalore of the Indian Institute of Tropical Meteorology (IITM) in 1985. This comprised of wind monitoring, wind mapping and complex terrain projects. The programme is today one of the world's largest wind resource assessment efforts covering 600 stations.

During the last fifteen years (1985-2000), the development of wind power in India went through three distinct phases, each marked by a paradigm shift in the policy and implementation frameworks. These are briefly brought out in the following paragraphs.

Paradigm I: Demonstration projects (1980 onwards)

Grid connected wind electricity generation, more famous as wind farms, started with the setting up of a demonstration programme of about 25 MW of aggregate capacity during the Seventh Five-Year Plan period (1985-90). Wind farms initiated during the year 1985-86 aggregated to an installation of about 3.3 MW capacity wind farms. During the same time, the Danish International Development Co-operation Agency (DANIDA) was the first international agency to show interest in the potential Indian wind power market, enabling the Danish manufacturer Micon to be the first to install wind power in India. In 1986, through a joint venture with Natural Energy Processing Company (NEPC) a 1.1 MW demonstration wind project was set up. Since then, a considerable level of interest was shown by international manufacturers of wind turbines, keen to gain a share of the large potential market for wind power in India.

Paradigm II: Indigenisation and private investments (1990 onwards)

The creation of a separate financial institution by the name of Indian renewable energy development agency (IREDA), in 1987 played a key role in facilitating renewable energy project implementation by offering loans on soft terms to users and manufacturers. The demonstration projects of grid connected wind electric generation started with more vigor, and efforts were being made to implement projects with higher rating (150 kW), than earlier ones of 50-100 kW.

One of the major objectives of the government through demonstration programme was to create conditions for the demand for such machines to grow so that indigenous industry could develop. Foreign wind electric generator (WEG) manufacturers started showing interest for collaborating with Indian companies for local manufacturing. Government, on its part, had devised an Import Policy allowing duty-free imports of WEGs. A private power policy for wind was also announced. However, no private sector investment in wind power occurred largely because investors were unsure of the economic response of the utilities, which were in poor financial health.

Paradigm III: Institutional reforms, re-structuring and commercialisation (1992 onwards)

During the early nineties, it was realized that faster diffusion of renewable energy sources required greater reliance on commercialization through fiscal rather than financial incentives involving the private sector - the role of the DNES had to change from an implementing organization to one facilitating the rapid commercial application of renewable energy. Partly as a result of this, the DNES was converted into a full-fledged Ministry (Ministry of Non-conventional Energy Sources, or MNES) in July 1992. After the formation of the Ministry, the thrust of the programmes has been on market development in order to facilitate and catalyze commercialization resulting in a several-fold increase in the diffusion of renewable energy technologies. India is probably the only country in the world with an independent Ministry for the promotion of renewable energy technologies (RETs) in the energy economy of the country.

In 1992, the MNES issued guidelines for electricity buy-back tariffs and banking. Some of the state governments also came out with incentives linked to sales tax benefits for corporates in the state. This set of investments, became the prime driver for investment in the post-1993 period.

Incentives for wind energy investors

- 100% accelerated depreciation on the equipment (MNES, 1992/1993)
- Concessional finance from Indian Renewable Energy Development Agency (IREDA) (2% less than the commercial terms, with an extended pay back time)
- Attractive buy-back rates, wheeling, & banking
- Third-party sales and sales tax exemption in some of the states

Post 1995-96: The Fall out & draw-backs

After the initial spurt in the wind power investment, there was a sudden fall-out in the investment (as shown in Figure 1), and table 1 below:

Table-1 : Yearly installed capacity

Year	*Installed capacity (MW)* *Demonstration*	*Private*	*Total*
7th plan	32	0	32
03/92	34.6	6.5	41.1
03/93	37.8	9.5	47.3
03/94	39.8	75.1	114.9
03/95	44	306	350
03/96	48.3	685.1	733.4
03/97	51.1	852.9	904
03/98	51.1	917.3	968.4
03/99	51.1	973.9	1025
03/2000	51.1	1049.9	1168
12/2000	57.1	1210.1	1267.2

(Source: Ministry of non-conventional Energy Sources)

The reason for a sudden fall-out, can be due to compounding of several reasons, as discussed below

Levying of MAT and lowering of corporate income tax

Wind investment enjoys 100% accelerated depreciation in the first year. This incentive led to high investment in wind projects in the initial period to offset the corporate income tax, otherwise to be paid by profit-making companies. This incentive was coupled with sales tax benefits in some of the states. In 1995/96, the then federal government lowered the corporate tax rate and levied MAT for zero tax companies. This led to lowering of tax credits. Independent of this development, some of the states started withdrawing third-party sales and sales tax benefits. Coupled with the general slowdown of the economy, it led to meager investments in the following periods.

Independent developments on the tax-credit front, led to the issue of negative cash flow during the loan repayment period, and resulted in the formation of non-performing assets in the wind power sector.

Mistrust amongst the investors

Early investments promised a capacity factor (plant load factor) in the range of 18-20% to the investors by the manufacturers. But, in reality the capacity factor was found to be as low as 8%-10% (Anand, pers. comm.), which led to more number of non-performing assets, as the revenue generation from the electricity sales was not able to meet the debt servicing to the finance companies

This had a bad impact on new investors and current investors who were planning to install more wind turbines.

Lack of proper power evacuation network

Power evacuation set-up is extremely important for ensuring higher capacity factor and revenue generation from the project. State Nodal Agencies have not been proactive in this direction. Sometimes power evacuation network cannot cater to the installed capacity of the site (which is much more), leading to downtime of grids, during high wind speed seasons.

A collaborative study carried out by TERI and ECN (Netherlands) (Rajsekhar et al., 1997) revealed the following facts

a. The combined installed capacity of wind farm in the coastal area of the state of Gujarat had exceeded 60 MW, but the power evacuating network could evacuate to a maximum of 35 MW.

b. Wind turbines have more downtime than the designed, due to high frequency and voltage fluctuations.

Lack of adequate maintenance infrastructure

Most of the sites where these systems are deployed are either far-off or cut-off from the main transport networks, due to which the manufacturers are not able to cater to the

O&M needs of the developer. This has led to private O&M services but needs are still felt for more O&M providers. In this respect, proper maintenance infrastructure and guidelines needs to be created for ensuring the reliability and higher capacity factor (capacity factor-equivalent to plant load factor).

Withdrawal of third party sales and sales tax benefits

Some of the states had provided third party sales and sales tax benefits, for wind farm investment. Over the years, most of the states have taken off such incentives. Also, in the light of the uniform sales tax policy adopted by the Government of India, all sales tax benefits for wind farm investment, have been taken off in retrospective from 1st January 2000.

Tax benefits and profitability in wind power sector

The presence of 100% accelerated depreciation (by the central government) and sales tax-benefits (at the state level), led to massive investment in the wind power sector in 1993/94 and 1994/95. The mechanism of which is quite easy to understand is as follows:

- An investing party (a profit making company) can off-set its tax by investing in wind power projects

Case-A (not investing in wind power projects)		*Case-B (investing in wind power projects)*	
Item	**Particulars**	**Item**	**Particulars**
Profit before tax	Rs. Y	Profit before tax	Rs. Y
Corporate tax-rate	40%	Corporate tax-rate	40%
Corporate tax paid	Rs. Yx 0.4	Wind farm investment	Rs. Y
Profit after tax	Rs Yx0.6	Corporate tax paid	Rs. 0
Asset generation	Nil	Asset generation	Rs. Y

- This was coupled with 50% and 100% sales tax benefits on the capital investment spread over 5-6 years, in different states
- Such a mix of incentive, make it lucrative to invest in wind power projects.

Levying of MAT

In 1995/96, the federal government introduced Minimum Alternate Tax for zero-tax companies, and also, the lowering of corporate tax by 5%. The Minimum Alternate tax was worked out at 33% of the corporate tax, hence, leading to lowering of tax credits for the investors in the wind power projects.

Case-A (not investing in wind power projects)		*Case-B (investing in wind power projects)*	
Item	**Particulars**	**Item**	**Particulars**
Profit before tax	Rs. Y	Profit before tax	Rs. Y
Corporate tax-rate	40%	Corporate tax-rate	40%
Minimum Alternate Tax	13%	Minimum Alternate Tax	13%
Corporate tax paid	Rs. Y*x* 0.4	Windfarm investment	Rs. 0.87*x*Y
Profit after tax	Rs Y*x*0.6	MAT paid	Rs. (Y*x*0.13)
Asset generation	Nil	Asset generation	Rs. 0.87*x*Y

Withdrawal of third-party sales

Coupling of tax incentives/breaks and selling of electricity generated to third party (industries), made it very lucrative for the wind power plant owners. Policy of third-party sales was viewed as a competition by the state utility boards, and led to lowering of energy sales to the industrial consumers. This led to the withdrawal of third-party sales in some of the states.

Negative cash-flow during the repayment period

Inclusion of MAT, withdrawal of third-party sales and sales tax benefits in some of the states, led to the formulation of negative cash flow during the repayment period. Such a development led to non-payment of debt/loan taken from different financial institutions by the wind power plant owners.

Windfarm as a captive power generation option

During the recession period (post-1996), the investment in wind power projects came mainly from the electricity intensive process industries. Such industries treat wind power projects, as a captive power generation station, to offset the heavy electricity bills.

Drawbacks

Wind power is not yet competitive with the conventional power generation systems, hence, incentives in some form are inevitable. The incentives for wind farm investment till now are investment linked (accelerated depreciation & sales tax benefits), and not linked to the performance of the wind farms. Consequently, the profitability/project viability was not much dependant on energy generation.

The investment-linked incentives, led to very high numbers of physical non-performing assets in some of the states. Hence, the investment in wind power plants became more of a balance sheet financing, than as an independent power project for energy generation.

Serious investors (process industries) have invested in wind power plants largely to offset the electricity bills by banking/wheeling the wind-generated electricity in the state grid. However, for large-scale commercialisation, the investor base has to increase; particularly of wind energy developers who sell electricity to the grid. Hence, proper policy framework for IPPs (Independent Power Producer) is a must.

Conclusions

It is important that power generation from wind needs to become competitive with coal-based electricity in the next five to seven years. This can be achieved through four broad policy aspects - stable policy environment, need for growth in demand, necessity to deal with the issue of buy-back prices, and institutional facilitation.

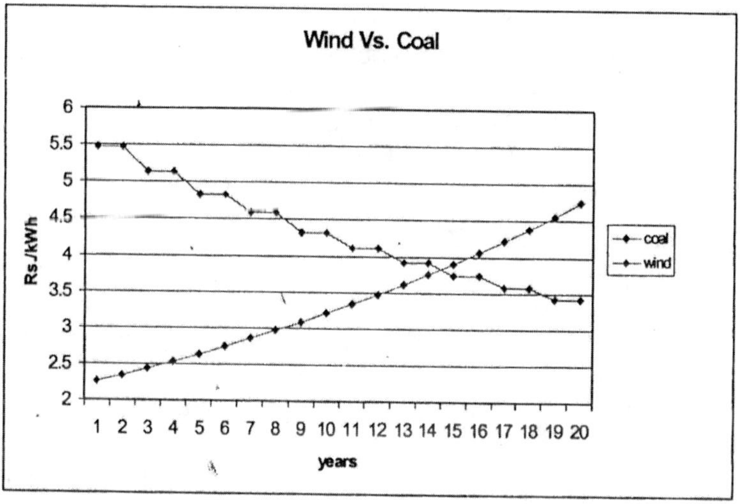

Stable policy environment

A stable policy environment is required to encourage the investors, the developers, as well as the financial institutions apart from IREDA for investing in the wind power sector.

There is a felt need for growth in demand. This can be achieved by associating a renewable energy block with every new power project.

The Electricity Supply Act and the Electricity Regulatory Commissions Act could also be amended to require all the state grid utilities to procure a minimum percentage of electricity from renewable sources on a competitive basis.

Better buy-back prices

The present electric supply structures are dominated by nationalised utilities, producing electricity from conventional thermal route based on coal or gas. Conventional power producing options employ fossil fuels, which in turn lead to local air pollution and GHG (Green House Gas) emissions at a global level. At present, there is no economic disincentive for conventional power producing options, which have adverse environmental impacts. A full cost estimate of coal-generated electricity triples the financial cost, rendering it more expensive than wind or biomass cogen.

Mechanisms such as economically efficient tariff setting and environmental disincentives for conventional power producing options are required in order to provide a level playing field for wind power generation. Alternatively, sufficient incentives should be given to make wind power a viable option. The regulatory commissions, envisaged under the Electricity Regulation Bill, should be charged with the mandate to incorporate environmental costs in the generation tariff, apart from ensuring transparency of costs in the pricing structure.

In the short run, buy-back at prices that are remunerative and promote efficiency fast enough to attain competitiveness is required. Also, a higher buy-back price during the initial years, especially when the loans are being repaid, is required for better project viability.

Institutional facilitation

Arbitrary changes that occur at the long of states, state policies, and various agencies in the state imply that for a stable policy environment, coordination and continuity is required. Single window clearance, right procedures, similar to those for mega projects, should be established. Projects of 5 MW or more can be considered as mega projects. A state sector task force or committee can be established to take care of various formalities.

Enhanced capacity building

Trained manpower to deal with the long term issue of maintenance and spares is of prime importance. Standards, certification, development of human resources, and help to the industry in terms of technological upgradation are very important issues in view of the limited cumulative experience in this field. This is important to ensure that quality of products and services is maintained, and investors' interests are protected.

Technological Development

It is necessary to create new markets for scale and efficiency; support and requirement for local indigenisation, adoption and upgradation and create testing and research facilitation.

Wind electric generators technology requires large financial and human-resource investment. This has occurred largely in Northern Europe, spurred by market growth there. Further investment to develop technologies appropriate for Indian wind regime, grid stability and climate will occur only as the Indian market enlarges. This implies that a policy regime that supports market growth and efficiency improvements is required. At the same time, research and upgradation support is essential. The creation of the Center for Wind Engineering Technology (C-WET) is the first step in this direction.

In the end...

In India, electricity liberalization is at a stage with no truly competitive markets. Where there are competitive markets, there are few sources of fuel and where the sources of fuel exist, they are badly exploited as in case of coal where the non-competitive industry, high cost, and poor quality raise the cost of alternative fuels. Traditionally, imported fuels are always priced just below what it costs in the domestic market to supply those fuels.

There are two main issues with respect to the supply aspect of wind power, namely improvement in capacity factor and reduction in cost. The responsibility chiefly lies with the wind turbine manufacturers. However, such efforts can yield benefits only if developers set up large projects and state electric utilities are convinced about the dispatchability of wind power.

Another important aspect is the divide between the manufacturers and developers (particularly in India). The whole wind power programme has been manufacturer driven whereas developers and consultants should have driven it. The manufacturer should be left alone to scale up the technology, drive down the cost, improve the capacity factor etc. The developer should be responsible for planning, designing, and developing the project.

References

Union Budget, 1995, 1996, 1997.

TERI, 1999. Wind Power: Experiences and Future Directions. July, New Delhi.

MNES, 1992/1993 Annual Report.

MNES, 1995/96 Annual Report.

Rajsekar, B., Chintan Shah, Dipti Gupta, (1997). *Grid Integrational Problems*. TERI, New Delhi

Personal Communication, Anand, S.K. IPCL, New Delhi

Plants in Delhi's Environment

10

Prithipalsingh

The Importance of Plants

Plants grow in almost every part of the world and influence the environment. We see some plants, flowers, or trees nearly every day. Without plants there would be no life on the earth. Plants are the primary food producers and suppliers of vital oxygen to the environment. Green plants are the only organisms endowed with the property of photosynthesis ("putting together with light") on this planet. By capturing sunlight, green plants are able to utilize carbon dioxide of the air and water from the soil to make food. This process also releases oxygen into the atmosphere, helping all organisms (including plants themselves) to respire.

Plants supply us with our basic needs of clothing and shelter besides food. The food we eat comes directly or indirectly from plants. Much of our clothing is made from plant fibers such as cotton. We use wood for house building and make many useful articles (including the paper on which this is printed) from several plant products. Many useful medicines are also obtained from plants. In addition, plants add beauty and pleasure to our lives. They are also used in various religious functions. People also enjoy the fragrance of flowers and the sights of natural landscapes. Plants are thus an integral component of our lives and the environment.

Before we appreciate the diversity of plant life in Delhi, it would be interesting to recall some information about this National Capital Territory of India. This city has witnessed fast unbalanced urbanization in the recent past, and has become a pampered area. All government agencies desire office and residential space and there is excessive commercialization. This information, along with knowledge about the geography, geology, climate and soils of Delhi, shall help us to understand the relationships between the plants and the environment of this region.

The Geography of Delhi

The national Capital territory of Delhi is a "narrow strip" of the Indo-Gangetic Plain. It lies between 28 °12′ and 28°53′ north latitude, and 76°50′ and 77°23′ east longitude. This region is bounded on the north, west and south by the state of Haryana, and on the east by Uttar Pradesh. The river Yamuna flows on its eastern border in a north-south direction. The area of Delhi is 1485 sq. kms. The greatest length of this territory is 51.90 km while the maximum breadth is 48.48 km (Chopra, 1976). This region is situated on the watershed dividing the two mighty river systems of northern India, the Ganges and the Indus.

The Ridge

The most prominent physiographic feature of Delhi is the "Ridge". This is the last spur of the Mewat branch of the Aravallis. The ridge enters Delhi from the south and extends like a "lean but wiry finger" straight to the Yamuna river. A branch of this hilly tract separates itself from the main path near Bhatti mines and extends in a north-easterly direction up to Arangpur. It then turns to the northwest and joins the main ridge in a sweeping curve. The irregular oval area enclosed by the 2 branches of the ridge, takes on the nature of a plateau.

The ridge can be classified or divided into 4 distinct pockets. (i) The Northern or Old Delhi ridge (now called Kamla Nehru Ridge) near the Delhi University Campus and bordering the Civil Lines extends up to the Yamuna river. It covers an area of about 87 hectares. (ii) The Central or New Delhi ridge extends from Dhaula Kuan in the south-east to Rabindra Rangshala in the north-west. It is flanked by Sardar Patel Marg on one side and extends to Rajinder Nagar. This also includes the Buddha Jayanti Park and the Mahavir Vansthali. The area of this pocket is 869 hectares. Raisana Hill, which was a part of this region, was selected for building the Rashtrapathi Bhavan and other government buildings. This imposing complex provides a grand/majestic view from the Rashtrapathi Bhavan to India Gate and beyond to the Yamuna river. (iii)Separated from the Old and New Delhi ridge pockets, is the south central ridge covering 626 hectares. This is more prominent in the Mehrauli-Vasant Kunj area. The Jawaharlal Nehru University Campus, the National Institute of Immunology and several other institutions are important landmarks built on this part of the ridge. (iv) The largest pocket is called the southern ridge. It is the actual last spur of the Aravallis and enters Delhi from Gurgaon in Haryana. This is spread over 6200 hectares. The total area of the Delhi ridge forms only about 6% of the landmass of this territory. This naturally green area, however, is the lifeline for the ever-growing population. It helps in maintaining the oxygen-carbon dioxide balance in the atmosphere, purifies the air we breathe, reduces noise levels, regulates temperature, and preserves biodiversity.

The ridge is fairly dissected. Storm water "nallas" have etched into its rounded-contours. For most part of the year, these channels remain dry. This inadequacy of water, as well as the rocky nature of the terrain, exert a great influence on the green cover of the ridge.

The average elevation of the ridge is about 215 meters above mean sea level. This is about 70 meters above the ground surface. The ridge, however, shows its maximum elevation of 318.5 meters near Bhatti. Interestingly, this point would be about 110 meters higher than the Yamuna railway bridge, which is used as a reference point for determining the flood situation in Delhi during the monsoon.

The Geology

The geology of a region influences the soil and this is very significant for development of vegetation. The rocks of Delhi belong to the earliest and latest chapters of the geological history of the earth, i.e. the Pre-Cambrian and the Quaternary. This is called the "Alwar Series" in geological terms. It consists of small hills, ridges and plateaus. The Ridge is one component of this series.

The Climate

The sub-tropical climate of this territory is characterized by a dry scorching summer (maximum temperature ranging from 43° to 47° Celsius) and a severe dry winter (minimum temperature 2-6°C) sandwiching a wet monsoon period (average annual rainfall 66.6 cm). It is influenced by various factors which affect the climate of the neighboring areas.

The Soil

Delhi's soil is a light sandy loam in most parts. It tends to get marshy during the monsoon. In the plains, the soil is alluvial, generally consisting of strata of silt, clay and sand.

The texture of the soil varies from coarse sand to clay. The alkaline soils are low in organic matter.

Thus, the geographical location, the subtropical climate of the area, the soil and other factors influence the plant life of this National Capital Territory. As one flies into the air terminal of this capital city, the majestic buildings catch the eye. These and the historic monuments, which are important landmarks, are dispersed in patches of greenery.

Delhi's Environment

Roonwal (1999) has presented an account of Delhi's 3000-year, history from Indraprastha to the National Capital Territory, and discussed various aspects of its environment. He has emphasized on the growth in its population during the past 50 years, the water supply to the residents of this expanding metropolis, and various aspects of pollution in this urban environment. His observations suggest that Delhi is an example of a complex urban system. In this context, it is necessary to understand the importance of plants in Delhi's environment.

The 'Master Plan Delhi 2001' approved by the government of India under the Delhi Development Act, indicates land use pattern. It clearly lays down the need to recognize the importance of large green areas. Besides this Master Plan, the natural green areas of Delhi also come under the purview of 2 major national acts: (1) "The Wildlife (Protection) Act, 1972" which defines National Parks, sanctuaries, etc. These are termed "Wild life areas"; and (ii) "The Indian Forest Act, 1927" which defines Reserved Forests (RFs), Protected Forests (PFs) and Village Forests (VFs or Gaon Sabha lands). These are called "Forest Areas". (Singhal, 1994). The following table provides information on some forest and wildlife areas of Delhi.

Table: Listing some forest and wildlife areas of Delhi as marked on Survey of India maps*

Name of area if any	Status	Survey of India map name/ no.	Square no/ s.	Description
1	2	3	4	5
Northern (old Delhi) Ridge (under DDA)	RF	Delhi guide map 53H/2	O6 & 7, P4-7 CI	Hilly area near the Delhi University, including Bara Hindu Rao Hospital, Mutiny Memorial, Flagstaff Tower, etc.
Central (New Delhi) Ridge	RF	Delhi guide 53H/2	K13&14, L11-14, M11-14, N10 &11 CI	Hilly area on both sides of the Ridge road, from Dhaula Kuan in the southwest through Rabindra Rangshala in the northeast includes Mahavir Vanasthali and Buddha Janathi Park, and the Polo Pavillion and Parade Ground.
Jahanpanah City Forest (under DDA)	PF	Delhi Guide map 53H/2	R21&22,S22 C3	Southwest of Greater Kailash-II and northeast of Madangir
Rajokri	PF	53H/2	B3	Next to Rajokri Village, off the Delhi-Jaipur Highway in South Delhi.
	PF	53H/2	A3	Next to Dhul Sira Village, east of the Najafgarh Drain, west of Bijwasan village in Southwest Delhi
Sultanpur	RF	53H/I	A3	Junction of Bawana Drain & Dabas Bawana Jhil Drain,

1	2	3	4	5
				near Bawana and Sultanpur Dabas village in Northwest Delhi.
	RF	53H/I	A3	Along Daryapur Drain, where it joins the Delhi Tail Distributary, near Gangatoli and Bawana in Northwest Delhi.
	RF	53H/I	A3	Near Ghoga and Bawana villages in Northwest Delhi.
	PF	53H/I	B3, C3	Near Mukhmelpur, about 2 km west of the Yamuna approximately 12.5 km north of Model town.
	PF	53H/I	B2	On the Delhi-Panipat Road, next to the Delhi-Haryana border, 3 km east of Narela, North Delhi.
Masudpur	PF	53H/2	B3, C3	Northeast of Masudpur village, Southwest of Munirka, JNU partially overlaps its.
Garhi Mendhu	PF	Delhi Guide Map 53H/2	R2 4 C1	East of Yamuna, south of Wazirabad Road

- The table is incomplete because the top sheets date back to 1970. Several RFs and PFs may have been notified since then. Also, several RF and PF areas are too small to appear at the scale of 1:50,000, (at which these top sheets are available). More detailed maps can be got from Survey of India, Dehradun. From : Singhal, 1994

The Plants of Delhi

The scientific study of plants of Delhi can be traced to the collections made by British botanists in the 19th century. John Forbes Royle, a pioneer plant explorer of Northern India, (Royle, 1833-1840) mentions about 55 species from the Delhi region Later. J.L. Stewart (1869) in his book "Punjab Plants" records 24 species from this 'District'. In 1918, R.N. Parker published "A Forest Flora of the Punjab with Hazara and Delhi" and mentioned 35 species of wild and cultivated plants from Delhi District. Later, Parker (1920) enumerated 67 species of wild and planted trees and shrubs on the Ridge. Amongst the Indian botanists, Singh (1945) collected economic plants occurring in Delhi Province while Mukherjee (1953) described the vegetation of Delhi ridge. The pride of place in floristic studies should however, go to Dr. J.K. Maheshwari. His intensive study of the flora of Delhi (Maheshwari 1957, 1963) has provided us with a taxonomic listing which has become an important source of information for plants of this region. The study of the vegetation of Delhi by Dakshini (1968) led to the collection of the various plant species as new records for Delhi by him and his research students (see Prithipalsingh & Sharma, 1999). A study of the trees of Delhi University (Ilyas, Kakar, and Mohan Ram, 1983) provides useful information. In addition, the NGO, Kalpavriksh, has also published an account of the Delhi Ridge Forest (Arora et al., 1991) and a citizen's guide for saving Delhi's green areas (Singhal, 1994). This information has helped us to understand many aspects of the plants of Delhi.

Most of the plants occurring on the ridge, in the valleys, on flat slopes, in marshes and ponds, and along the river banks are naturally occurring. Many other plants, though not indigenous, have become naturalized. An ecological analysis of the information about the plants of Delhi indicates that trees are sparse, of medium size, and form an open canopy. This offers sufficient scope for a dense herbaceous ground cover. The low rainfall and the gravelly substratum do not support any dense perennial vegetation. Thus, for most part of the year, the climate and soil conditions favour a semi-desert vegetation.

In addition to the natural flora, much of the greenery of Delhi is contributed by the plants grown in gardens, parks, along avenues, traffic roundabouts, and in the areas under agriculture. Some aspects of the plant life of Delhi are discussed in the following paragraphs.

The Ridge Forest

This is one of the world's largest city forests and this natural vegetation of Delhi is botanically described as a "scrub forest". It constitutes the most important green area of this territory. It is a tropical thorny secondary forest. The northern and central pockets of the ridge have been defined as reserve forests. The floristic composition of these 'ridge forests' can be studied under two categories: (i) the permanent vegetation, and (ii) the ephemeral vegetation.

The Permanent Vegetation

The permanent vegetation of the Delhi ridge consists of thorny tree species and a few scrub species. Acacia species (commonly known as Babul, Khair, Wattle,etc.) dominate the tree group. Prosopis (Vilayti or Kabuli Kikar) is the co-dominant member. The other conspicuous tree members distributed in the area include Salvadora (Pilu), Balanites (hingot), Azadirachta (Neem), Butea (Flame of the Forest; Dhak, Palas or Tesu), and Ehretia (Papri). The wild date palm (Phoenix) occurs in a few isolated clumps. The chief shrub components of the permanent vegetation are Capparis (Karira or Kanthari), Zizyphus (Beri), Cordia (Indian cherry), and Grewia (Phalsa). The glycodin plant (Adathoda vasica) is a very common gregarious under shrub co-dominant with Capparis. In the depressions on the ridge, the shelter and shade supports species such as Anogeissus pendula (Dhao), Diospyros cordifolia (Tendu), Jaminum multiflorum (yellow Jasmine), Tecomella undulata (Wave-leaved Bignonia), Securingea leucopyrus (Hartho) and Zizyphus numularia (Beri), All these species are typical plants of the Aravalli system.

The Ephemeral Vegetation

The ephemeral component of the vegetation, consisting of annual herbaceous plants, comes up mostly during the monsoon season. The easy availability of moisture, both in the soil and in the atmosphere, promotes rapid growth of these short-lived annuals. Many common herbs and several grasses grow easily. Climbing and twining plants (which get support from the thorny shrubs of the permanent vegetation) also contribute to the seasonal vegetation. After the monsoon season, these plants gradually die and are replaced by winter season annuals. The grasses are again very prominent along with a few chickweeds.

The Riverine Tract

Besides the ridge forest, plants growing along the banks of the river Yamuna add to the biodiversity of Delhi. The sandy and alkaline soils support a rich vegetation after the monsoon and during winter. Some of the common plants are the butter cup (Ranunculus), the slivery weed (Potentilla), the water pepper (Polygonum), the toad rush (Juncus), the Kans (Saccharum), the loonak (Salsola), the alkali seepweed (Suaeda), and the jhau (Tamarix).

A rich aquatic flora can also be collected from ponds, puddles, and marshy areas, especially after the monsoon. Many interesting hydrophytes add to the plant component of Delhi. The more common ones are the duckweed (Lemna), the Indian water lily (Nymphaea), the water chestnut or Singhara (Trapa), the Indian reed-mace (Typha), the Bengal terror (Eichhornia) and the eelgrass (Valisneria).

The Weeds

Apart from the plants of the ridge and the Yamuna banks, several other species occur as weeds. These 'camp followers of agriculture' occupy varying habitats and form a group of their own. They represent an important section of the herbaceous plant cover of Delhi. Many of these species produce a great number of viable propagules and withstand the vagaries of the climate. In each season, characteristic weeds appear in almost every habitat. The common weeds include the amaranths, the spurges, the legumes, and many grasses. These weeds occupy all available pockets or niches along roadsides, in wastelands, in orchards, and in gardens. They break the monotony of the habitat and add greenery to the surroundings.

During the last 30 years or more, the author has observed changes in the species composition in the natural vegetation as well as the spread of weeds. On one hand, several species not recorded in the Flora of Delhi (Maheshwari, 1963) have been collected from this region. Additions to the Flora of Delhi include Heliotropium curassavicum (Dakshini 1970), Cotulla australis (Dakshini & Vijayaraghavan, 1970), Bidens bipinnata (Dakshini & Prithipalsingh 1971), Soliva anthemifolia, Centipeda minima, and Merremia emarginat a (Dakshini, Prithipalsingh, and Maheshwari, 1973), Hewittia bicolor and Digitaria stricta var. stricta (Aggarwal, Nayar and Dakshini, 1976). At the same time, some species reported by Maheshwari (1963) are no longer found in the region. Some of these are Caesulia axillaris, Zexuine streumatica, Orobanche aegyptiaca, Utricularia species, and Leptadaenla pyrotechnica

The recent fencing of the northern ride has also led to a change in the floristic composition. Thus, Lantana camera is becoming more prominent and it is preventing the growth of other plants. A similar change is also taking place in the other fenced off areas of the central ridge. The noxious carrot weed or ' congress grass' (Parthenium hysterophorus) has also assumed a menacing position and has spread widely. It occurs along roadsides and in open places, dominating the herbaceous vegetation and preventing the normal growth of other plants.

Similarly, during my early visits to Okhla in 1967 and 1968 for my investigations on the Compositae of Delhi (Prithipalsingh, 1969), it used to be a common sight to find the pteridophyte, Equisetum (horse tail), growing luxuriantly. Individual stems of this plant measured more than a meter in length. But, now when I accompany my students to botanise the same area, we find this plant occurring only in small patches. They have a stunted appearance and individual stems are usually 10-15 cm long only. These and other changes in the composition of the vegetation are indicative of the change in Delhi's environment.

The Cultivated Plants of Parks and Gardens

The addition to the natural flora, much of the greenery of Delhi is contributed by the cultivated plants grown in parks, gardens, along avenues and traffic roundabouts. The residents of Delhi were proud of the Lodhi gardens, the Roshanara Bagh, the Nicolson Park, the Mughal Garden of the Rashtrapati Bhawan, the Teen Murti House surroundings, the Delhi University Campus, and other important places where plants are grown in an aesthic manner. To these were added the elegantly landscaped area of the Rajghat complex, the well-laid out Buddha Jayanti Park and several neighborhood parks developed by the diversified activity of the Delhi Development Authority. The area beyond the Rajghat on the Ring Road towards the Yamuna Bridge has been developed into a species-rich "Shanti Van" which has been classified as a 'Reserve Forest'. In addition, several 'city forests' have also been developed. The'Jahanpanah' (literally, one who gives shelter to the world) is one such city forest (southwest of Greater Kailash part II, near Chirag Dilli towards Madangiri). Recently, "Smriti Vatikas" have been developed near Chanakyapuri and other places where one may plant trees in memory of loved ones. Similarly, the "Mahavir Vanasthali" has been developed in a part of the Central or New Delhi Ridge. All these along with the private residential gardens especially in "Lutyen's Delhi" and in the Delhi cantonment area are also important. The recent development of gardens in farm houses has helped in introducing many new plant species to Delhi.

The cultivated plants include trees, shrubs, and ornamental annuals. The older more mature trees are native species with a wide spreading canopy. They not only provided welcome shade especially during summer, but also provided a majestic appearance blending well with their surroundings. Some of these like the Neem (Azadirchta indica), the Jamun (Syzygium cumini), the Semal (Bombax ceiba) and others have a productive, medicinal and social value. They were adapted to the environment and provided livelihood to the less fortunate members of the society. Other native speices grown in Delhi include the 'Kachnar' or 'Camel's Foot Tree' (Bauhinia), the 'Sacred Barna' (Crataeva adansonii), the 'Krishna Vat' (Ficus krishnae), the Bael (Aegle marmelos), the 'Peepal' (Ficus religiosa), the palas or Tesu (Butea monosperma), and many more. Along with these native speices, many exotic species have also established themselves. Thus we come across the 'Silver Oak' (Greviella robusta), the 'Sausage Tree' (Kigellia pinnata), the 'Gulmohar' (Delonix regia), the 'Amaltas' or Golden shower (Cassia fistula), the 'Bottle brush' (Callistemon), the 'Shaitan' or scholar's tree (Alstonia scholaris), the 'Floss Silk tree' (Chorisia speciosa) and many more, with Eucalyptus being found in almost all parts of Delhi. Besides these, fruiting trees such as mango, loquat, guava, tamrind, pomegranate, and even jack fruit are also grown.

A large number of botanically interesting plants have been introduced into the Delhi University Campus by Professor KMM Dakshini during his tenure (1975-1987) as Secretary of the Garden Committee. Many of these have attained maturity and are flowering. Some of the these are listed here.

Botanical Name	Common Name	Botanical Family
Adansonia digitata	Baobab Tree	Bombaceae
Adenanthera pavonina	Coral wood or Red Bead Tree	Leguminosae
Amoora walichii	Amari timber	Meliaceae
Bassia butyracea	Indian Butter Tree	Sapotaceae
Bursera delpechiana	Linaloe or Lignaloe Tree	Burseracea
Cinnamomum camphora	Camphor Tree	Lauraceae
Colvillea racemosa		Leguminosae
Diospyros ebenum	Ebony	Ebenaceae
Flindersia sp.	Australia Timber	Rutaceae
Gynocardia odorata		Flacourtiaceae
Heptapleurum sp.		Araliaceae
Holarrhenna antidysenterica	Kurchi	Apocynaceae
Kleinhovia hospita	Bola	Sterculiaceae
Koelreutaria Paniculata	Copper Bronze Ttree	Sapindaceae
Manilkara hexandra	Khirni	Sapotaceae
Parkia Africana		Leguminosae
Ochna squarrosa		Ochnaceae
Quercus sp.	Cork Oak	Fagaceae
Sapindus mukorossi	Soap nut Ttree	Sapindaceae
Tabebuia sulphurea	Trumpet Flower Tree	Bignoniaceae
Terminalia meyesi		Combretaceae
Terminalia myrocarpa	Hollock Timber	Combretaceae
Toona ciliata		Meliaceae
Triplaris surinamensis		Polygonaceae

Besides the native and introduced tree species, a large number of shrubs also add greenery and colour to the landscape. Th more common shrubs grown in various parts of Delhi include the 'Chandani' (Tabernaemontana divaricata), the 'Bellyache bush or Bherenda" (Jatropha) the 'Golden dew drop" (Duranta), the "yellow elder" (Tecoma), the "yellow oleander or Pili Kaner" (Thevetia) and many more. In addition to these, a riot of colours attracts every one when the numerous ornamental annuals bloom in all their glory from mid February to mid March. This is the best time for admiring the beauty of plants in Delhi.

All kinds of annuals are being cultivated now. Beautiful carnations, gladioli, dahlias, buttercups, salvias, marigolds, pinks, stocks, roses, gerberas, tubelilies, asiatic lilies, and even tulips are now occupying coveted positions in floral decorations. The desire to present floral bouquets to friends and relatives on various occasions has led to the mushrooming of florists in bazaars and along roadsides. This has added a new dimension allowing everyone to admire the beauty of nature's gifts to mankind. As in the case of changes in species composition of the natural vegitation, there is a gradual drift in the kind of cultivated tree species being planted. Instead of trees with a majestic appearance and large canopy, small exotic trees with a very insignificant spread are being planted in large numbers. We come across the 'Ashok' (Polyalthia), the 'Australian Acacia' (Acacia auriculiformis), the 'Pagoda Tree' (Plumeria) and others along roadsides, in gardens and other places of recreation.

Thus, on analyzing the overall picture, we find that there is a blend between the natural vegetation and the cultivated plants. The plant cover of Delhi comprises of nearly 1000 species. About 60% of these are indigenous or naturalized and the remaining 40% are either introduced or cultivated. This may give an impression that Delhi environment is endowed with many plant species. But statistics alone do not make up the complete picture. The quality of plant life is important, and it is here that we should be concerned about. Environmental degradation due to various factors has had an adverse effect on plant growth. Urbanisation and its associated pressures on available land has affected the environment in many ways. In addition to this, the survival of many avenue trees is now being threatened by the high levels of atmospheric pollution and concretization of pavements. There is an urgent need to arrest the deterioration and loss of Delhi's greenery. The awareness that green plants alone shall ensure our survival in this metropolis should awaken everyone. Although, fast unbalanced urbanization has taken a toll on Delhi's environment the awareness being generated by the activities of NGO's concerned with Delhi's green areas is making the citizen aware of the need to conserve the green areas. Therefore it is hoped that "the Jahanpanah City forest" and other such protected areas shall give shelter to Delhi's greens and thus protect the environment.

References

Arora, A., Bagla, P., Hazarika, N., Kothari, A., Lal, R.Menon, S., and Shahabudin, G. (1981), the *Delhi Ridge Forest*, Kalpavrikash, New Delhi.

Aggarwal, S.K., Nayar, E.R., and Dakshini, K.M.M. (1976), Distributional Records of Hewittia bicolor and Digitaria stricta var. stricta. *Acta Botanica Indica*, 4: 157-158.

Chopra, P. (ed) (1976), *Delhi Gazetteer*, Gazetteer Unit, Delhi Administration, Delhi.

Dakshini, K.M.M (1968), *Vegetation of Delhi State*: Mehrauli Region I: Analysis of Pattern, Proceedings of National Institute of Sciences in India, 34: 127-133.

-- (1969), Distributional Records of Two Taxa in Northern India, *Current Science* 38: 117-118.

-- (1970), Heliotropium Curassavicum Linn: An addition to the Flora of Northern India, *Journal of Bombay Natural History Society*, 66: 660-61.

-- *et. al.* (1973), Distributional Records of Soliva Anthemifolia, Centipeda Minima and Merremia Emarginata in and near Delhi. *Current Science*, 42: 396-397.

Dakshini, K.M.M and Vijayaraghavan, M.R. (1970), Cotula Australis (Sieb. Ex Spreng.) Hook. F. A., New Record for Northern India. *Indian Forester*, 96: 24-25.

Ilyas, M., Kakar M. and Mohan Ram, H.Y. (1983) *Trees of Delhi University Campus*, pp. 16-30

In: Bhatia, S.C. (ed), *The Environmental Concern*, Centre for Adult and Continuing Education, University of Delhi, Delhi.

Maheshwari, J.K. (1957), *The Flora of Delhi*, Ph.D. Thesis, University of Delhi, Delhi.

– – (1963), *The Flora of Delhi*, Council of Scientific and Industrial Research, New Delhi (reprinted by INSDOC, 1976)

Mukherjee, S.K. (1953), Vegetation of Delhi State, *Journal of Bombay Natural History Society*, 51: 439-465

Parker, R.N. (1918), *A Forest Flora for the Punjab with Hazara and Delhi*. (2nd ed. 1924, 3rd ed. 1956). Superintendent Printing, West Pakistan, Lahore. Reprinted: Bishan Singh Mahendrapal Singh, Dehradun, 1994.

– – (1920), Afforestation of the Ridge at Delhi, *Indian Forester*, 46: 21-28.

Prithipalsingh (1969), *Compositae of Delhi: A Re-investigation*, M.Sc. thesis, University of Delhi, Delhi.

Prithipalsingh and Sharma, R. (1999), Publications of Professor K.M.M. Dakshini, pp. 13-22. In: Tandon, R.K. and Prithipalsingh (eds), *Biodiversity, Taxonomy, and Ecology*, Scientific Publisher (India) Jodhpur.

Roonwal, G.S. (1999), Delhi: An Example of Complex Urban System, pp 315-326. In Tandon, R.K. and Prithipalsingh (eds), *Biodiversity, Taxonomy, and Ecology*, Scientific Publishers (India), Jodhpur.

Royle, J.F. (1833-1840), Illustrations of the Botany and Other Branches of the Natural History of the Himalayan Mountains and of the Flora of Cashmere, London.

Singh, H. (1945), Some Useful Wild Plants of the Delhi Province, *Indian Journal of Agricultural Science*, 15: 297-308

Singhal, G. (1994), Saving Delhi's Green Areas: *A Citizen's Action Guide*, Kalpavriksh, New Delhi.

Stewart. J.L. (1869), *Punjab Plants*, Lahore Government Press; Reprinted, Bishan Singh Mahendra Pal Singh, Dehra Dun.

Overview of Human Impacts on the Coastal Ecosystem

11

Ganpat S. Roonwal

Introduction

To give an overview of the issues of human impacts on coastal ecosystem is interesting. Though I have not been trained in land use planning, I am by training a geologist, the bulk of my experience having been in terrestrial issues or deep-sea exploration. During 1986-90, I studied the coastal environment of certain parts in Orissa state. Therefore, my interest in coastal zone issues triggered off in 1988 when I was asked by the Department of Ocean Development (DOD) to contribute an article relating to coastal zone study (Dwivedi et al., 1989). Thus I become a part of the multi-sectoral team, which reviewed the likely socio-economic implication of changes in the Indian coastal zone.

Furthermore, in 1992, I guided a research work on the Chilka Lake, which comprised of a study of very delicate ecosystems. And during the process, I had the opportunity to meet representatives of various multi-sectoral institutions in Orissa state. It has been confirmed through our field experience in Orissa that the institutional marine sector of their economy is weak in decision-making. I have unfortunately no knowledge or experience of either western coast of India, or further south on the east coast, but I am convinced that the same institutional constraints of compartmental and line thinking, inherited from the past colonial regime would also persist there perpetuating the schism in real communication that exists between the areas and that, unless checked, is likely to maintain a constant threat to the long-term sustainability of our coastal ecosystem which are in the highly vulnerable zone.

The other main issue, which is relevant here is the limited perception at the policy level of the long-term threats to the sustainability of coastal ecosystems by terrestrial activities. The coastal waters are often readily and openly used as a sink. What is not readily visible to the naked eye does not have an impact and furthermore there is a dearth of baseline data and monitoring in respect of the coastal environment.

The limited perception can be traced back not only to decisions made at local/district level, but also to those with regional (and even international) collaboration, it being a well known fact that an institution such as the World Bank, that has funded heavy infrastructure project (ports etc.) in the region has only begun to incorporate environmental concern into their thinking since the late 1980's.

Furthermore, although higher learning and research institutions have now been established in the Orissa coastal zone, the fact that marine science initially received low priority has subsequently created cumulative setbacks in terms of relative numbers. Therefore, the relative impact that can be made upon localized decisions of terrestrial activities is small. The linkages between marine science and policy makers have been limited.

The support for environmental strength of coastal areas would also not be forthcoming from local communities due to poverty issues (recent starvation deaths in Orissa shows the level of poverty). Unless people can have time off from survival issues, they cannot be expected to care and fight for the environment. Moreover, the communities have insufficient awareness of the complexities of the various interrelationships.

Yet, events which have been taking place in Orissa (and possibly others areas) such as the serious environmental degradation brought about by the polarization effects of the coast, and the continued use of the coastal waters for sink function dictate otherwise, and this has been discussed in this paper.

The modification of terrestrial areas, on the coast and upstream has a high potential for advance effects on coastal ecosystems and the linkages are such that it is not possible to have effective management of coastal resources without a concurrent management of local habitats, with the specific objective of coastal management stewardship in mind.

To begin with, let us look at the specificity of the area we are referring to.

The Coastal Zone: Specification

The coastal zones constitute some of the world's most productive areas. The offshore sectors provide valuable marine resources including high protein food, while the onshore sectors feature amongst the most sought after areas in terms of residential settlement and trade as well as other business opportunities.

The definition of the coastal zone can be as elusive as that of sustainable development. There can be several definitions. In the context of this article, the boundaries would need to be tailored to capture major coastal zone management issues.

In some areas, depending on geographical features, the inland boundary could be quite narrow. In others, it could reach extensively inland. Generally, however, such boundary could include, all coastal areas that are subject to storm flooding by the sea, all inertial areas of mangrove, marsh, deltas, salt flats, tide flats and beaches; and permanent shallow coastal water areas such as bays, lagoons, estuaries deltaic waterways and near coastal waters, that include sea grass meadows, coral reefs, shellfish beds, submerged bars, the near shore coastal waters and all small coastal islands.

To focus more specifically on the Orissa region, we note that tropical marine environments are characterized by high species diversity which is less tolerant of change in surroundings. The sum effect of their characteristics generally results in tropical organisms and communities being more susceptible to disturbance or pollution than their corresponding counterparts in temperate seas.

Human Impact of the Coastal Zone

The coastal zones the world over are the focus of much developmental activity. It has been an inevitable process since the days of exploration and the setting up of maritime links and trade throughout the world. More than half of the world's population lives within 60 km of the coastal line and this figure in predicted to rise to three quarters by the year 2020. In India, the coastal development process has been accentuated by the growth of export-oriented economy since the early days. Many of the ports which are there are also the state capitals, the business and industrial centers, such as Kolkata, Mumbai, Chennai, and Kochi and Vishakapatnam, to mention just a few. These create job opportunities, while the hinterland often extending down the coast, is the area for additional shelter, food, and fuel as well as the dumping ground for waste disposal. Parts of the marine area are also used as convenient dumps.

Ineffective planning and management of coastal zones, the absence of environmental impact assessment, inadequate incorporation of environmental issues into feasibility, population pressure as well as increased economic activity are threatening the integrity of the natural ecosystems. All over the coast of India, there are examples of coastal research which are leading to diminishing return as well as the degradation of environmental quality.

We shall now look further into the human impact issues of the coast.

The Coastal-pull and Urbanization

Stewardship of the coastal environment and its critical ecological system has to reckon with trends, and therefore the coastal pull factors as well as rapid urbanization that exists within our region. Factors contributing to this coastal pull could be various and include for example, the existence of traditional ports (Kakinada Tuticorin, Vasco de Gama, Kolkata etc.) which in turn have created multiple other opportunities, and in turn attract more and more people from the hinter land, alternative economic opportunities based on the exploitation of the beauty of the coastline and leisure opportunity (Goa, Kerala), fishing opportunities and influence of people from inland to the coast due to adverse conditions (drought etc.).

Within India, this coastal pull would be compounded by the strong urbanization process that typifies our region and shows a rapid rate of growth. The urbanization process itself is a heavy resource consumer and in view of the pressure of population and poverty as well as the absence of effective urban management, is not very caring towards the environment. In our context, it is over-exploitation that commonly extends the construction of shelter and accompanying infrastructure, both basic and social, into new areas, often without adequate forward planning. The inability to manage and cope with increasing waste, stemming from rapid urbanization, magnifies the problem of coastal pollution.

Land development involves substantial resource use not only in terms of land unit area, but also in terms of natural materials which go into the building of the shelter and the infrastructure needs.

Exploitation of Non-living Marine Resources

The exploitation of beach placer deposits on the east and west coasts is an example of a marine resource with important economic as well as ecological functions, which is heavily used in the overall urbanization process (Gopalpur – Orissa and Kerala beach placers) of the coastal environmental balance and quality.

The need for cyclone proof housing in Orissa, for example, has caused significant sand depletion in various areas, accentuating coastal erosion and increased risk of flooding. Yet, sand extraction is incompatible with beach conservation, essential for a tourist-oriented economy.

Tourism

Other economic opportunities such as tourism development or major industrial infrastructure are also resulting in over-exploitation of coastal resources. Coastal tourism is dependent upon the beach for its infrastructure and upon the adjoining coastal waters for its recreation.

Tourism is, however, in a unique position. Whilst it is exploiting the natural resources of the coastline, it is also dependent upon the continued quality of that physical raw material for its own survival. Therefore, the tourism sector is generally more vigilant and caring in its approach. In the absence of a strong urban management structure with appropriate enforcement and pollution control, industry has been traditionally much less concerned with environmental stewardships and its processes often feed upon the drawing of clean water from aquifers or surface reservoirs and the disposal of solid wastes, often of unrevealed composition, into disposal areas which find their way eventually into the sea. This is discussed next.

Disposal of Waste Waters

The disposal of urban and industrial waste waters into the coastal waters creates perhaps the most significant loading factors that the marine environment has constantly to rekon with. Industrialization results in highly toxic effluents being discharged, directly into the bays and lagoons, later reaching the ocean.

Solid Wastes

In our region, solid wastes are often disposed in dump sites, with little funds available for sanitary landfills. Some of these sites are directly on the sea (Headland Sada, Goa), but even›where they are not, leakage and seepage can result from the convergence of pollutants to waterways and eventually to the sea. Solid wastes are not taken seriously.

Intensive Exploitation

Urbanization and the concurrent growth of population in quest for fuel, and food, also gives rise to further intensification in the use of solids. In India, the primary use is agriculture. Destruction of forest (including mangroves) for fuel and clearance for agriculture places and additional strains on vegetation cover and solids are disrupting ecological balances. Population pressure combined with the shortage of agricultural inputs induces malpractices which in turn lead to increased soil erosion and siltation problem. Subsequently, the siltation process finds its ways to the sea, smoothening coral reefs with serious consequences for fishing and tourism. Agricultural practices making use of chemicals induce agrochemical pollution. The deployment of pesticides and fertilizers has not been accompanied by adequate environmental awareness.

Manipulation of Hydrological Cycle

Construction of dams for the storage of water and for the harvesting of hydroelectric power is taking place throughout peninsular India. They are valued projects in view of the tangible benefits which are achieved. However, there are definite negative impacts in so far as the marine environment is concerned, relating to the total trapping of alluvial sediments which results, in sediment supply impoverishment at river mouth and deltas. This induces recession of shorelines and can have an impact upon the spawning and growth cycle of marine fish and prawn species as well as upon fisheries further off-shore.

Marine Transport of Oil and other Hazardous Substances

Another major hazard comes from the passage of oil tankers concerned with the transportation of oil along the Indian ocean region and coasts. Visual observation of offshore oil slicks are seen along the Indian coastline near Bombay. Indian efforts of surveillance has helped in the safe and clearing of tar balls on beaches in the polluted area.

The possibility of oil spill from one of the large tankers moving through the route in the Arabian Sea, the Andaman Sea, and the Bay of Bengal is the biggest single environmental threat to the marine environment as a whole. Oil threatens the environment in many ways and oil slicks can poison aquatic life and smoother corals. As oil breaks down, its chemical components affect the feeding and reproduction of many organisms. Chemical dispersants, used to break down oil slicks, can create another form of pollution. Further more, huge cargo of hazardous material being transported long distances are a real threat to marine life and ecosystems.

Exploitation of Living Marine Resources

Within the coastal zone of all the coastal states in the Indian union, fishing is a victim of pollution rather than a source of it. However, the fact remains that utilization of marine resources takes place without concern for the interaction between different components of the marine environment.

Two major issues must be mentioned (1) the industrial fishing carried out by both Indian and foreign fishing fleets have negative effects on habitats and stocks, and (2) the over-exploitation of marine resources attributable to rising human population, degradation of land and shortage of land-based jobs and in short, the depletion of resources and the poverty cycle. This induces malpractices, including use of dynamite for fishing off the coral reefs, which is another serious cause of concern. The explosions smash the coral and destroy the habitat of fish and other reef-dwelling organisms. Through repeated blasting over a period of time, extensive areas of coral reefs are destroyed and the fisheries productivity of the reefs decline.

A new popular area of intervention is aquaculture development. But these need to be closely monitored it the light of the harmful affect through accumulation of food waste, at the bottom, which could lead to nutrient overloading.

Issues

This overview of human impacts upon the coastal ecosystem brings to light the following major issues:

- The coastal zones constitute some of India's most productive areas in terms of fishing and the living resources, and other non-living resources, agricultural production, leisure opportunities as well as business and other economic opportunities. But the productivity and quality of these coastal zones in seriously threatened by the degradation caused by human activities and rapidly increasing population growth.
- Many of the ecological areas are highly sensitive to change. Under normal condition of development, such critical ecological units adopt to nature, but when the rates of change are rapid, adaptation is difficult and there can be serious environmental degradation.
- Activities carried out on land have a strong bearing upon the coastal environment. Depending upon relief factors, this influence can extend fairly extensively inland. As long as the human population was low, nature could keep pace and remain sustainable.

- There are now concerted government efforts to make awareness of the coastal zone system. New restrictions proposed would, it is hoped, help in keeping nature/ human balance.

What could be done is to train the staff responsible in (a) general aspect and (b) specialist aspects – environment management plans, science linkage, public awareness, through community partnership, legal and institutional framework to attain the set goal of integrated coastal zone management.

Reference

Dwivedi, S.N., V.S. Bhatt and P. Chaturvedi (Eds.) (1989), *Coastal Zone Management in India*, New Delhi: Indian Association of Advancement Sciences.

PART-IV

Conceptual Issues

Lack of Basic Environmental Infrastructure in Slums and the Ecological Footprint of the Urban Poor

12

Anjali Bhardwaj

Introduction

Since 1950 urban population has grown from under 17% of the world's population to approximately 50% in 2000. It is estimated that 90% of future population growth will be in urban areas and most of the growth is likely to be among the poor (UNICEF, 1997). While urban settlement patterns have varied across countries, in no country have efforts to restrain migration or urban growth been successful.

The forces contributing to urban growth are strong and are closely linked to the process of industrialization and development. Higher urban wages reflect the higher productivity of labor in cities where economies of scale and agglomeration have made households and enterprises more productive. This productivity growth, although beneficial, has not solved the massive urban problems of the developing world, and serious issues of urban poverty and a deteriorating urban environment remain. Many households have not found employment and income-generating activities, and many live in squatter areas unserved by essential infrastructure. Even if the poverty is still largely rural in many countries, as the 1990 World Development Report concludes, urban poverty will become the most significant and politically explosive problem in this century making the current pattern of development highly unsustainable in the long run.

Experience in developing countries like India shows that the larger a city the greater the proportion of slum population. Growing urban slums and social, economic and environmental problems associated with them have recently caught the attention of development agencies and governments. According to publications of the Urban Management Programme (UMP) set up by the UNDP/ World Bank/ UNCHS, the critical and most immediate problems facing developing countries are impacts of urban pollution that derive from inadequate water supply, sanitation, drainage and solid waste services and high levels of air pollution. Collectively dubbed the 'brown agenda' this set of problems is closely linked to the poverty-environment nexus.

Ecological footprint definition

The concept of the Ecological footprint developed by Prof. Wackernagel, Director of the Indicators Programme, Redefining Progress, San Francisco, measures human impact on nature. Because humans consume the products and services of nature, everyone has an impact on the planet. The "ecological footprint" concept has been designed to estimate people's impact on the environment. It does this by measuring how much nature people use to sustain themselves. The ecological footprint of any defined population is the total area of ecologically productive land and water occupied exclusively to produce all the resources consumed and to assimilate all the wastes generated by that population, using prevailing technology. As people use resources from all over the world and affect far away places with their wastes, footprints sum up these ecological areas wherever that land and water may be located on the planet.

Slum dwellers are not a high consumption group but the extremely poor environmental condition of slums shows that the urban poor do have a substantial environmental impact. Unlike the economically better off sections of population the large ecological footprint of slum dwellers is not due to their high levels of consumption but rather due to lack of basic infrastructure available to them. This paper looks at how factors related to lack of basic environmental infrastructure in developing country slums lead to a high ecological footprint of the urban poor and what possible solutions exist that would reduce the footprint. Since close to 40-70%of the population of cities like Delhi, lives in slums/ slum like conditions (Rawal, 1998), the discussion of the ecological footprint of slums is to discuss the environmental impact of a large fraction of the urban population of developing countries.

Lack of basic environmental infrastructure in slums

Slums in cities of most developing countries are characterized by poor physical infrastructure facilities such as solid waste disposal, water supply, sewage disposal and drainage, thus leading to problems of severe environmental degradation. Lack of basic environmental infrastructure in slums leads to a disproportionately higher environmental impact of slum dwellers as compared to their levels of well being. This section discusses the environmental problems associated with poor infrastructure availability in slums which lead to a significant ecological footprint of slum dwellers.

Environmental problems arising from lack of appropriate waste collection mechanisms and waste disposal sites in slums

The quantity of solid wastes generated per person per day in the urban areas in developing countries like India has been reported to be roughly 250- 300g depending on socio-economic and cultural habits of the people, urban structure and density of population (Holmes, 1984). Slum dwellings/ households do not have large open spaces where waste can be stored. This poses problems in adopting a house-to-house collection system. Due to low purchasing power, people are not able to purchase and maintain standardized waste containers and municipal administrations are reluctant to provide these containers due to the large capital cost and effort involved in purchasing and maintaining an inventory. Household waste is thrown randomly in the drains and the streets outside the houses which leads to severe environmental degradation and related health problems. In order to dispose waste, many households collect their rubbish and burn it thus releasing considerable amounts of CO_2 and particulate emissions.

The environmental ramifications of poor solid waste collection mechanisms and lack of proper waste disposal sites in slums include drainage and leachate problems, ground water pollution which leads to severe problems as handdug wells and shallow handpumps are a common and important source of water for the slum dwellers (Ali, 1990). Also, irregular waste dumping leads to fields getting converted into dumping grounds not conducive for anything to grow on. Rains take waste to drains, causing them to be blocked thereby creating water-logging and ground water pollution. In addition, waste is the origin of pungent odours, especially in the hot season and the appearance of the town is unsightly. Wastes dumped in streets favours the development of infectious environment related diseases such as dysentery, worms, enteritis, typhoid, hepatitis and cholera and burning of waste adds to air pollution in the city.

Environmental problems related to inadequate water supply facilities

Slums do not only have low levels of access but also poor quality of water. Formal supply is generally subsidized unevenly among the different income groups, hence not only is there disparity in water supply coverage, but also in the accrual of the benefits of the subsidy.

The problem of water theft arises due to lack of sufficient water supply. The urban poor break water pipes at various places in order to get drinking water which leads to puddle formation and other associated environmental hazards as discussed below. Even when water is supplied to certain areas, very often the slum dwellers install pipes to take water upto their dwellings. The pipes are poorly maintained and are usually found leaking at various points. It is common to find animals drinking from points at which pipes are broken to steal water. The problem is further aggravated by the fact that often water and sewage pipes run close to each other and many sewage pipes leak. Thus the water that is eventually consumed by both the slum dwellers and the non poor gets severely contaminated and causes the outbreak of epidemics and diseases (Sarda, pers. comm.).

Water leaking from ill-maintained and broken pipes as a result of poor maintenance and water theft respectively, gets mixed with various pollutants and seeps into the ground causing ground water pollution. Eventually the same polluted water is consumed by the urban poor since most handpumps from which they procure water are shallow and thus provide polluted water (Ghosh, pers. comm.). Apart from diseases caused due to polluted drinking water such as hepatitis, cholera and typhoid, leaking water mixes with waste and causes human diseases such as malaria and dysentery through the insect breeding that waste disposal encourages.

Environmental problems caused due to lack of drainage and excreta disposal systems

Since slums are usually situated on totally unserviced land they have no drainage and sewage networks servicing them. Therefore they are characterized by water clogging and associated problems especially after rains. Often, the only form of drainage in most slums is a network of small open drains joining a large open drain. These drains are very poorly maintained and often get clogged due to solid waste disposal directly into the drains. This implies that the drains overflow and cause water logging in large adjoining areas. When the big drain gets blocked all the water from it flows back into the small drains and causes sewage and waste water to flow into the slum dwellings. Thus the slum dwellers have no choice but to manually unclog the big drain thereby exposing themselves to serious health hazards.

The disparity between lower and upper income levels in terms of sanitation facilities is generally very significant. Flush latrines connected to the sewerage system are common in the higher income brackets. As in the case of water supply, subsidized sewage facilities are often available to relatively well off sections of the population who not only have the privilege of latrine facilities but also their exclusive use. The pattern for poor households is just the opposite, with slum dwellers having limited/ no access to sewage facilities. For instance in 1993, over 42% slums in Delhi did not have access to any toilet facilities (Bhushan, 1999).

Poor drainage and sewage facilities lead to ground water and drinking water pollution. Slums are characterized by foul smells emanating from rotting waste and open drains carrying sewage and refuse of the urban areas. Added to this is the problem of open defecation due to non-availability of proper toilet facilities. All these factors combined lead to stench and unsightly appearance of the slums. Drainage of waste water into open drains provides the most readily identifiable health risk, namely that of promoting the breeding of *anopheles* and other mosquitoes. In areas of seasonal rainfall where the drains are liable to be blocked, the addition of excreta and waste water creates year round standing water and thus year round mosquito breeding where seasonal breeding would otherwise occur.

Many important infectious diseases are associated with human excreta. The most common association is that the pathogens causing the disease leave an infected person by way of the faeces or urine. One gram of human faeces may contain 10^9 infectious virus particles, regardless of whether the individual is experiencing any discernible illness (Richard *et al*, 1983). Excreta are therefore the direct source of these infections. Human excreta are the principal vehicle for the transmission and spread of a wide range of communicable diseases (over 50). Four groups of pathogens – viruses, bacteria, protozoa and worms cause these diseases some of which rank among the chief causes of sickness and death in societies where poverty and malnutrition are ubiquitous.

Diarrhoea, respiratory diseases, endemic malaria, meningitis, dysentery and malnutrition are the main causes of death among small children and infants in developing countries. Cholera is accompanied by numerous deaths in all age groups. Other diseases such as hookworm infection and schistosomiasis, cause chronic debilitating conditions that impair the quality of life and make the individuals more liable to die from superimposed acute infections.

Work in China and the US in the 1920s and 30s showed that poor families who used their latrines and prevented their children from defecating in the yard had significantly lower intensities of Ascaris infection than their neighbours (Bradley, 1992). Therefore, the collection, transport, treatment and disposal of human excreta are of the utmost importance for the health of any community.

Programmes to improve the environmental conditions of slums

There is increasing awareness that slums are not self contained compartments - stench emanating from unserviced dumps forms part of everyone's physical environment, diseases caused due to these neglected services do not stay contained within the confines of the slums as slum residents often work as domestic help in non-poor households. These factors coupled with the increasing number of slums imply that it is imperative to take action to improve the environmental problems associated with urban poverty.

A number of programs have been adopted for the improvement of the environmental conditions of the urban poor by different governments and development agencies. However given the widespread nature of the problem, more needs to be done. Some measures that have been adopted by developing country governments for the environmental improvement of slums are:

a. ***Relocation of squatters:*** This programme has usually not been very successful as adequate land is not available for relocation. Also, often relocation is to the periphery of the city which adversely impacts the family's income earning capability.

b. ***In situ slum upgradation:*** In this system the slum dwellers are not dislocated from their original places. The government demolishes the existing dwellings and divides the area into plots of land which are given to the original inhabitants after providing all basic infrastructure facilities such as street lighting, sewage pipes, drainage facilities, water supply etc. The slum dwellers then build the houses on the allotted plots.

c. ***Environmental improvement of urban slums:*** Basic infrastructure facilities are provided to slums according to certain set norms such as financial limit of a certain amount, one water post per 150 persons, one toilet seat per 20-25 persons, large dustbin at regular intervals etc. There are financial constraints on undertaking these activities.

As discussed earlier, the lack of basic environmental infrastructure in urban slums leads to a significant adverse impact on the environment. This section discusses the possible solutions that can be adopted by developing country governments and development agencies to provide adequate infrastructure to slum dwellers which would reduce the ecological footprint of the slum dwellers while simultaneously increasing their level of well being.

Suggestions to ensure effective waste collection and disposal in slums

In the case of urban slums, testing and adopting the most effective waste collection and disposal mechanisms assumes tremendous importance. The municipal governments need to introduce and test the most suitable waste collection and disposal methods. The most widely used system in developing country urban areas, wherein storage bins owned and maintained by civic authorities are provided at frequent intervals along the roadside can be extended to service slums (Ali, 1998). The points to be borne in mind are:

- In order to prevent refuse from being deposited indiscriminately, depots must not be located too far from the slum or be placed anywhere not easily accessible
- It is important to employ depots of the right capacity and ensure regular emptying

Best/most suitable practices of waste collection and disposal can be drawn upon from international experience. For instance, the Chinese employ the principle of mass participation for both refuse and night soil collection. The refuse vehicles visit residential areas at specific times of the day and make a familiar sound. People bring out their waste to be emptied into the vehicles. If backed with proper health education of the public, the system is likely to work in most of the developing countries. World Bank solid waste projects in India, Indonesia and Egypt use pushcarts as a principal mode of house-to house collection within the lowest income neighbourhoods - this is tied to improvements in the basic infrastructure of specific low-income neighbourhoods.

Another way of reducing the ecological impact of the urban poor is by composting their wastes. Currently only a small fraction of the waste from urban areas in most developing countries is composted, the rest goes into sanitary landfills or is tipped in surface water bodies. As in China where 90-95% of the total waste (sewage and refuse) produced is employed to make compost to enhance agricultural production, simple and labour intensive methods of composting could be employed to reduce costs. This would also reduce the need for chemical fertilizers, thus decreasing the ecological footprint of the slum dwellers (Holmes, 1984).

The main factor which makes efficient solid waste management difficult is shortage of funds. Since refuse disposal does not generate any revenue and environmental health programmes are not always high among the priorities of public authorities in developing countries and refuse disposal is rated far below water supply or housing, it is not surprising that refuse disposal is often poorly funded (Schubeler, 1996). Allocation of more funds for waste disposal is crucial.

However, the experience in most developing country cities indicates that even when large sums are spent on sanitation, services rendered are far from satisfactory due lack of co-operation by citizens and ineffective planning. The system needs active co-operation and participation of citizens. This can be achieved only when people become aware of the ill-effects of the existing systems and the advantages of using proper methods. Any kind of efficient collection system almost certainly requires a change of householders' habits. This is likely to be even more difficult than organizational improvements. Where it is customary to throw rubbish 'outside the front door' or at the corner of the street, people usually accept the resulting mess as part of their inevitable environment. Environmental education of the population is thus important and should cover all segments of the population from school-going children to senior citizens.

Solid waste management is an urban issue, the level of government responsible is typically local or metropolitan government. Solid waste management is a public good since it possesses qualities of being nonexclusive, unrivalled and essential. However, this does not mean that the local government has to accomplish the task of solid waste service delivery entirely with its own staff, equipment and monies.

This is where the role of the private sector comes into play (Cointreau-Levine, 1994). The project of solid waste disposal should be guided by the basic idea that those who cause the waste should bear the costs of its disposal. User charges as one means to cover solid waste cost should not be ignored. They give the solid waste agency some autonomy by eliminating the need to compete with all other government agencies for their share of general revenue. User charges also render the solid waste agency more directly accountable to residents for the services they provide. In communities wherein the residents have been sensitized to the need for public cleanliness and to the problem of limited resources (or efficiencies) of government, the door to door collection service can be treated as a private good for which those being serviced would be willing to pay. Private sector firms are motivated by profits, therefore they could make the system of collecting waste and user charges efficient. The private sector can charge an appropriate fee from the slum dwellers in accordance with the willingness to pay (WTP) which is often underestimated (L.N. Sharma, pers. com.).

Currently, even at high levels of expenditure the level of solid waste service is low and no more than 50-70% of the solid waste is collected (Bijlani *et al*, 1991). This is due to poor management of waste disposal bodies. Solid waste employment roles are bulging with extra employees, many who are scarcely productive and others who do not produce at all. One of the most frequently cited advantages of the private sector over government is its management flexibility and efficiency. It has greater ease in firing personnel for non performance and in providing upward mobility for workers with good performance. Good management, supervision and labour relations make a great deal of difference.

The methods of private sector participation most common to solid waste management are contracting, franchise and open competition. Among the various options for private sector participation, contracting for solid waste service hold the greatest promise to developing countries as a way of lowering cost. Even when only a small portion of the city is served under private contract, significant efficiencies may be achieved because of contestability of market principles, wherein the government monopoly over service delivery is contested. Based on studies conducted in 317 cities in England and Wales and in 126 cities in Canada, contracting of solid waste collection service was 22% to 41% - less costly respectively – than public service (Holmes, 1984). Those cities in which a private contractor provided refuse collection and thus eliminated public monopoly, costs were lower.

However solid waste activities such as refuse disposal can have significant spillover, that is, water and air pollution can migrate from the area of service to surrounding area. It is thus not advisable to decentralize disposal to local governments within a metropolitan area or to private markets unless the regulatory framework and sanctions are adequate.

Informal sector solid waste collection: It is possible for governments to work with community groups, NGOs, and co-operatives for improving solid waste services. It is worthwhile for the government to explore organizing collectors into a co-operative and developing a franchise arrangement whereby the rights and responsibilities of the informal sector collectors are defined. It needs to be borne in mind that to the problem of waste management there are no universal solutions, every slum needs a system tailor made to its own physical and economic environment.

Possible solutions for providing adequate water supply to slums

Governments must not shy away from providing the very basic of services to slums. It is extremely important to adopt a scientific approach to supplying water to these communities. Intelligent and need based engineering becomes highly important. Also, careful planning of water and drainage pipes is essential. The two sets of pipes running close to each other cause health hazards in case of leakages.

According to one school of thought, privatization of water and sanitation systems is inevitable as the forces of demand coupled with willingness to pay shall compel a move towards privatization of infrastructure facilities. The government does not have enough resources to ensure the provision of all basic facilities to people. The already meagre funds are going to prove to be even more insufficient in the face of rapidly increasing urban populations. The final solution to the problem is likely to be private agencies providing water and sanitation services against user charges which ensure cost recovery.

In designing any slum water supply systems, it is important that the starting point be a well designed market survey of demand for water by the urban poor who often have much higher ability and willingness to pay than is assumed by water agencies. A high level of community participation in the planning, implementation, operation and management as well as collection of charges, of water supply systems will ensure that supply will be better targeted to community demands.

Suggestions for providing adequate drainage and toilet facilities for slums

The most obvious constraint on sanitation is the cost of latrines. Since the urban poor have financial constraints and are settled on illegal land not serviced by sewers, the existing distribution of sanitary facilities is skewed towards the rich. Even when toilets are provided in slums they are usually not suited to the needs of the users.

Excreta disposal systems must be suited to the slum's environmental conditions – the climate, endemic diseases, water availability, culture – many of which are clearly beyond the control of public authorities. To do this requires that a planner have a good "feel" for the slum dwellers' culture and preferences. User preference and acceptance should be explored in every project in which the acceptability of the technology is the least bit in doubt. Any excreta disposal system is a complex social activity involving planners, administrators, politicians, and corporation workers as well as the individual users (World Bank, 1998b).

The location of latrines is important and must balance advantages. People may be sensitive about issues like the prominence of the toilet to public view, and such factors must be evaluated in detail for each situation. For instance mobile toilet van facility has been unsuccessful in many cases as slum dwellers find it too conspicuous and therefore embarrassing to use. If the latrine is sited at some distance from the living quarters, people may be discouraged from using it on dark nights or in inclement weather. Yet if it is close to the house there may be a feeling that defecation is not adequately segregated from the rest of daily living. In a project in Chennai in India where toilets were provided in each flat it was found that some of these were filled with sand and the space used for other purposes. One explanation was that defecation within these small apartments even behind closed doors was unacceptable to the occupants (Moser, 1997).

Creating community awareness is extremely important for extensive use of toilet facilities or else even if toilets are installed they are not used. Due to lack of awareness, the slum dwellers do not consider using toilets a priority and therefore are not willing to pay for the use of the toilets.

Provision of basic services such as sewage and drainage pipes linked to network is an absolute must both for the welfare improvement of slums and to decrease the environmental impact of slum dwellers. There are international agencies like DFID and the World Bank spending or preparing to spend large sums of money to improve this situation.

The effective maintenance of open drains and toilets is extremely important. The solution to environmental problems caused due to open drains is either to use an alternative method of waste water disposal or to prevent drains from blocking by covering them and by vigorous efforts to keep them clear. The latter approach may be more realistic and can be implemented by employment of municipal workers by sub contracting the job to the private sector or by organizing and motivating community effort on a neighbourhood basis (Sharma, pers. comm.).

Relevance of NGOs in reducing the environmental impact of slums

NGOs can play a pivotal role in the context of environmental improvement of slums discussed above as they can effectively address 'brown issues' such as sanitation, drainage, waste management and air pollution by ensuring that communities are strengthened and mobilized to take action. They can facilitate the formation of Community Based Organizations (CBOs) by creating awareness among slum dwellers.

It is increasingly being recognized both by governments and international donor agencies that since it is the NGOs/CBOs that finally work at the micro level in slums, they are the best equipped to understand problems plaguing slum dwellers and also often in the best position to offer and help implement solutions at the micro level. No two slums are alike and therefore a common set of prescriptions is not likely to be very effective and solutions need to be adapted to suit each slum's specific requirements. Therefore any successful management programme, be it poverty alleviation or environmental improvement, needs the support of the local NGOs in order to be successful and sustainable (Bhatnagar, 1991).

When environmental infrastructure improvement measures are implemented it is often desirable for the beneficiaries to be closely involved in the process and to contribute towards the initiative in monetary terms. This is of great importance as:

i. The complete involvement of the community and the financial stake they perceive in the project ensure that investments go into the relevant/desired areas

ii. Since the community has a financial stake in the project, residents feel more responsible for the maintenance and upkeep of the facilities and thus the project becomes sustainable.

These factors ensure the sustainability of infrastructure and environmental improvement projects (Narayan, 1995). NGOs can play an instrumental role in mobilizing the community to contribute financially and be actively involved in the planning and implementation of the project. At the planning stage, NGOs can help identify the specific needs of the beneficiaries so that the project can be planned to provide what the slum dwellers need and what is suitable for their specific requirements. By motivating slum dwellers and explaining to them their responsibilities and rights and by helping create institutions in the slum such as sanitation committees etc the NGOs can help ensure proper maintenance of facilities provided and hence the long term success of the activities undertaken.

Research shows that environmental conditions in slums where there is no NGO presence are much worse than those where NGOs have been working for several years. All these factors point to the fact that there is need for strong yet informal micro level organizations such as NGOs and CBOs if sustainable efforts towards environmental improvement are to be made in slums.

NGOs can play an extremely instrumental role in imparting environmental education and awareness among slum dwellers. Despite remarkable availability of facilities in urban areas, illiteracy in slums is often as high as 40-70%. In a revealing study of several squatter slums in Delhi, as many as 91% of slum dwellers were found illiterate and 80% parents wanted their children to help in domestic work and earn money rather than go to school (Sivaramakrishnan, 1991). In such a situation, it is not surprising that the level of awareness among slum dwellers regarding the health impacts of poor sanitation, inadequate drinking water supply, use of toilets etc is extremely poor. NGOs can thus play an important role in the environmental improvement of slums by educating and sensitizing slum dwellers to some of these issues.

Conclusion

Developers the world over are being confronted with rapidly growing, politically powerful squatter communities. The growth of urban slum areas mirrors the growth of cities. Urban growth on the current scale has a major environmental impact especially in neighbourhoods where the installation of critical infrastructure is lacking.

As discussed earlier the 'ecological footprint' concept estimates the impact on the environment of any defined population (from a single individual to a whole community or country). It is the total area of ecologically productive land and water occupied exclusively to produce all the resources consumed and to assimilate all the wastes generated by that population, using prevailing technology. Ecological footprint calculations are based on two facts: first, it is possible to keep track of most of the resources consumed and many of the wastes generated; secondly, most of these resource and waste flows can be converted to a corresponding biologically productive area.

The spreadsheets used to calculate ecological footprint of populations have been developed keeping in mind the well off population of the world residing in developed countries having access to all basic facilities. Environmental problems like environmental health hazards, foul smell and problems such as those arising from water theft, cannot be easily quantified. Though slum dwellers are not a high consumption class, due to factors such as lack of basic infrastructure facilities and density of population, their environmental impact tends to be large although not easy to quantify. Unlike the more affluents sections of society for whom high consumption levels are the cause for their large ecological footprints, it is this unquantifiable factor that is really relevant in any analysis of the ecological footprint of slum dwellers. This unquantifiable factor needs to be tackled by environmental managers to reduce the environmental impact of the slum dwellers. The options, therefore, that environmental managers need to concentrate on in order to reduce the ecological footprint of slums are the solutions to the lack of infrastructure facilities in slums.

The slum dwellers in some ways are the highest return bracket for investment in environmental improvements in the short run (Parker *et al*, 1995). This is because, the affluent population groups have a large environmental impact due to their high consumption patterns and any attempt at reducing these, other than an increase in energy efficiency, is perceived to be a reduction in their level of well-being and is therefore not welcome. The kind of behavioural change/adjustment that is needed is unlikely to take place quickly and can easily be reversed. However, investments as small as Rs 1500 ($35) per capita in infrastructure coupled with good management and sound policies will not only reduce the environmental impact of the urban poor but also vastly improve their level of well-being. This exercise will therefore be welcome and aided by the communities themselves (Bijlani *et al*, 1992). Also, while many developing countries believe that they are unable to afford high environmental standards, Sonmez and Curi argue strongly that over the long term developing countries cannot afford not to have them because of the high costs of dealing with environmental disasters such as outbreak of epidemics, ground water pollution etc (Parker et al, 1995).

Also, it is worth mentioning that due to the overall inadequacy of services in the city, it is seen that even minimal improvements in water supply, drainage or sanitation cannot be carried out and sustained in the slums in isolation from significant improvement in city-wide infrastructure. Proper waste collection, provision of sewers etc in slums is important but it would be incorrect to assume that this alone would reduce the ecological footprint of the urban poor. If this waste is not properly disposed, it would only imply a relocation of the problem to another site.

Slum dwellers are decidedly not the highest consumption class in any country and therefore one cannot contest the fact that while addressing their environmental impact one is looking at only a fraction of the entire ecological footprint of the city. Yet the endeavour of this paper is to show that despite the low level of well-being of slum dwellers, their ecological footprint is much larger than need be, due to the lack of availability of basic physical environmental infrastructure facilities.Thus environmental improvement of slums holds the potential of being a win-win proposition from the environment-development point of view. Ensuring provision of adequate environmental infrastructure facilities to slums and encouraging the role of NGOs and CBOs will not only decrease the ecological footprint of the slum dwellers but also tremendously increase their level of welfare and quality of life.

References

1. Aggarwal, A. (1998), *Down to Earth*, November 30, 1998, Centre for Science and Environment.
2. Ali, S. (1990), *Slums within Slums*, Delhi; Council for Social Development.
3. Ali, S. (1998), *Environmental Scenario of Delhi Slums*, Delhi; Council for Social Development.
4. Bhatnagar, B. (1991), *Non-Governmental Organisations and World Bank supported Projects in India: Lessons Learned*, Asia Technical Department, Departmental Papers Series, No 2. New Delhi; World Bank.
5. Bhushan, B. (1999), Evaluation of accessibility and adequacy of Basic Amenities in Urban Slums and EWS bustees: Policy issues and Agenda for Future. Delhi; Ministry of Urban Affairs and Employment.
6. Bijlani, H.U., Roy, P. (1992), *Slum Habitat - Hyderabad Slum Improvement Project*. Delhi, Council for Social Development.
7. Bradley, D., Stephens, C., Harphan, T., Cairncross, S. (1992), *A Review of Environmental Health Impacts in the Developing Country Cities*, Urban Management Programme Policy, Paper 6. Washington, D.C.; World Bank.

8. Cointreau - Levine, S. (1994), *Private Sector Participation in Municipal Solid Waste Services in Developing Countries*, Urban Management Programme Policy, Paper 13. Washington, D.C.; World Bank.

9. Holmes, J.R. (1984), *Managing Solid Wastes in Developing Countries*, Wiley-Inter Science.

10. Khosla, R. (1997), "Slums and infrastructure", *Urban Poverty;* A Quarterly Newsletter of the National Institute of Urban Affairs, January-March 1997.

11. Khosla, R. (1998), "Problems in Slums", *Urban Poverty;* A Quarterly Newsletter of the National Institute of Urban Affairs, July-December 1998.

12. Moser, C. (1997), *Household Responses to Poverty and Vulnerability*, Urban Management Programme Policy, Paper 21, Washington, D.C.; World Bank.

13. Narayan, D. (1995), *Designing Community Based Development*, Environmentally Sustainable Development, Participation Series Paper No. 007, Washington, D.C., World Bank.

14. National Institute of Urban Affairs (1991) *Basic Services and Urban Poor*, Delhi; National Institute of Urban Affairs.

15. Parker, R., Kreimer, A. and Munasinghe, M. (1995), *Informal Settlements, Environmental Degradation and Disaster Vulnerability*, Turkey, World Bank.

16. Rawal, Y.P. (1998), *Slums in the Capital City*, Delhi, Government of Delhi.

17. Richard, G.F., Bradley, D.J., Garelick, H., and Mara, D.D. (1983), *Sanitation and Disease - Health aspects of Excreta and Wastewater Management*. World Bank Studies in Water Supply and Sanitation 3, Great Britain ; John Wiley and Sons.

18. Schübeler, P. (1996), *Participation and Partnership in Urban Infrastructure Management*, Urban Management Programme Policy, Paper 19, Washington D.C.; World Bank.

19. Sivaramakrishnan, K.C. (1991), "India", *The Urban Poor and Basic Infrastructure Services in Asia and the Pacific, Volume 2*, Manila, ADB.

20. UNICEF (1997) *Women and Children in Urban Poverty-What Way Out?* Geneva, UNICEF

21. World Bank (1992), *Development and the Environment, World Development Report* 1992, Washington, D.C., World Bank.

22. World Bank (1996c), *World Development Indicators*. Washington D.C.; World Bank Publication.

23. World Bank (1997a), *India - 1997 Economic Update: Sustaining Rapid Growth*, Delhi, World Bank.

24. World Bank (1997b), *India - Achievements and Challenges in Reducing Poverty*, Washington, D.C.; World Bank.

25. World Bank (1998b), *India - Water Resources Management Sector Review; Urban Water Supply and Sanitation Report, Volume I*, Delhi; World Bank.

26. World,Bank (1998c), *India - Water Resources Management Sector Review; Urban Water Supply and Sanitation Report, Volume II*, Delhi; World Bank.

Personal Communications

Aggarwal, Anil	Director, Centre for Science and Environment (CSE)
Akbar, Sameer	Specialist, Environment Unit, World Bank, New Delhi
Chandrakant	Deputy Director, Slum Cell, Ministry of Urban Development, Government of India
Datta, Tapas	Project Officer, UNICEF
Ghate, Anjali	Director, Deepalaya Jagdamba Camp Slum Project
Ghosh, P. K.	Under Secretary, Ministry of Urban Development, Government of India
Gurpreet	Liaison Worker, National Institute of Urban Affairs
Howes, Stephen	Senior Economist, Poverty Reduction and Economic Management Unit, World Bank, New Delhi Office
Jha, A. K.	Deputy Secretary, Ministry of Finance, Government of India
Kenny, Simon	Project Officer, DFID India

Khosla, Renu	Project Officer, National Institute of Urban Affairs
Rawal, Y. P.	Deputy Director, Slum Wing, DDA
Richardson, D.	Professor, Integrative Biology, Patterson Lab, University of Texas
Sarda, Dr. N.	Doctor, Safdarjung Hospital, New Delhi
Sharma, L. N.	Deputy Secretary, Poverty Alleviation, Ministry of Urban Development, Government of India
Tripathi, Yogendra	Deputy Secretary, Water & Sanitation, Ministry of Urban Development, Government of India
Wackernagel, Dr. M.	Director of the Indicators Programme, Redefining Progress, San Francisco

Firm Location in a Spatial Model with Pollution

13

Yamini Gupt *

Introduction

Pollution in water bodies and in the air has always fascinated economists. A popular example of a pollution externality is of firms polluting nearby water resources such as rivers and streams. In doing so, these firms impose damages on downstream users of the resource. Baumol and Oates (1988), Kamien, Schwartz and Dolbear (1966), Kneese (1964), Kneese and Bower (1968), Tietenberg (1996) and Gupt and Veendorp (1997) are some authors who have used this example.

Pollution in a water body like a river or a stream is transmitted in a linear space. The Hotelling model (1929) and several of its extensions study firms and consumers in a one-dimensional setting by distributing them along a linear market.

* The author wishes to thank Prof. E.C.H. Veendorp (Dept. of Economics, Clark University, Worcester, M.A., USA) for his insightful comments.

This market could be along a village main street or in a mountain valley with a river flowing alongside. Given this scenario, a firm located upstream along the river and discharging waste into it would impose an externality on a downstream firm using water from the river. The downstream firm would then have to incur an additional cost to clean up the water it uses. The interaction between these Hotelling-type firms is affected by the presence of the pollution externality (Gupt and Veendorp; 1997 a and b).

Several authors such as Coase (1960), Wellisz (1964), Nutter (1968), Tybout (1972), and Marchand & Russell (1973) have used a scenario with a price taking firm imposing a negative externality on another in their discussions of the Coase theorem. These examples, however, do not allow for duopolistic interaction between the firms selling their (differentiated) product in the same market. Among the few authors who have dealt with externalities in an oligopolistic setting, Levin (1985) analyzes an externality affecting the demand side of the market, and Veendorp and Zambaras (1992) consider Cournot type oligopolists generating an externality that affects all of them in a symmetric fashion. Germain (1989) is probably the only one who looks at one duopolist imposing an externality on another, but the competition among the duopolists is still of the Cournot type.

Gupt and Veendorp (1997a) incorporate the idea of externalities in the Hotelling setting and look at firm location decisions in fixed-price variable location and variable-price variable location models (1997 b). Their model has an upstream duopolist polluting a river and thereby imposing an externality (in the form of an additional clean up cost) on its downstream competitor. There is a uniform distribution of consumers along the market who have an inelastic demand for the good produced by the firms. The pollution externality affects the consumers through an increase in transportation cost (pecuniary externality). The firms enter the market in the manner described by Prescott and Visscher (1977). The authors find that in the fixed-price model, the firms locate asymmetrically under different liability regimes and internalization of the externality and taxation are not effective options to ensure the socially optimal location. Site regulation is suggested as a policy option. In the variable-price, variable-location model, the authors find that both firms might even prefer a more polluting technology to a less polluting one under certain liability scenarios.

This study extends the work done in the earlier papers by allowing a continuous location choice under different liability rules. It analyzes the impact of different parameters on the location decision of the firms when the price is exogenously determined and attempts to find a suitable policy option to minimize the pollution and total social cost associated with the externality and ensure sustainable development.

The Model

The model in this study incorporates the idea of externalities into spatial competition. The externality is modeled as the clean-up cost incurred by a downstream firm which uses water from a river polluted by an upstream firm. The presence of the externality affects the location decisions of the firms. For certain parameter values and locations of the firms, the externality can create a non convexity in the social cost set and lead to a local minimum instead of a global one.

Location could mean the physical position of a firm in geographic space or in characteristic space. When the physical position of firms is considered in geographic space, consumers choose to buy from the firm at whose site the price and transportation cost is minimized. In characteristic space, the consumer's location implies his/her ideal product or characteristic. The distance between the firm and consumer would then signify the difference between the brand characteristic considered ideal by a consumer and the characteristic actually purchased. The physical location of the firms in geographic space would be the same as in product space if the product characteristic under consideration was the location of the firm. However, in this model location is only interpreted as the physical position of the firms in geographic space which affects the transportation cost incurred by consumers.

The socially optimal locations of the firms are those at which the total cost to society is minimized. In the presence of the pollution externality, firms are likely to locate at positions other than socially optimal ones. The externality imposed on the downstream firm in the form of pollution is *technological* in nature. The consumers in this model are also affected by the externality, albeit indirectly. The less than optimal distance between the firms forces them to pay more in transportation costs. This increased cost would seem akin to a *pecuniary externality.*

The model uses the Hotelling framework, in which the products of the two firms are identical except for the locations at which they are sold. The Hotelling model assumes a linear market with a uniform distribution of consumers who consume a unit of the commodity in each unit length of the market, and incur a transportation cost per unit of distance. There are zero costs of production and no consumer has a preference about a seller except on the basis of price and transportation cost. In order to sell, each producer's price must not exceed the other's by more than the cost of moving the product between them. The social optimum would then require minimizing the transportation costs which implies locating the two producers symmetrically in the market at the quartiles.

The firms enter the market in the sequential manner described by Prescott and Visscher (1977). In the first sub stage, the first firm enters the market and the second firm enters in the second sub stage. The second firm is aware of its rival's location and the first firm correctly anticipates where its competitor will locate. Both firms maximize their profits given this information and the knowledge that no other firm will enter the market. The focus of the model in this study is on the location decision of the firms, and the price is assumed to be exogenously determined like in Eaton and Lipsey (1975). The consumers therefore patronize the closest firm. A fixed-price scenario is selected in this study, because it eliminates the instability caused by price competition. The fixed price could be a consequence of regulation or of competition from other firms located along nearby rivers.

The Pollution Cost

The cost of pollution, or the cost incurred by the downstream firm to clean the river water it uses is positively related to the output levels of the firms and the intensity of pollution which characterizes the production technology in use. The distance between the firms has a negative effect on the pollution cost. Conventional wisdom suggests that pollution cost should decrease with the distance between the firms. Rivers and other water bodies have an inherent capacity to assimilate pollutants. This assimilative capacity depends on the type of pollutant, the temperature of the water and other factors like the time pattern of stream flows and the location of waste discharge. Organic pollutants are broken down by bacteria which increases the biological oxygen demand. Authors like Thoman (1972) and Ortolano (1984) have used first order decay functions to estimate bacterial concentrations in rivers.

The properties mentioned in the preceding paragraph are incorporated in the following pollution cost function:

$$PC = \gamma \frac{q_A^{\alpha} q_B^{\beta}}{(k + x_B - x_A)^{\delta}}$$

where γ is the pollution cost coefficient which measures the intensity of pollution; x_A is the location of the upstream firm; x_B is the location of the downstream firm; q_A is the output level of the upstream firm; and q_B is the output level of the downstream firm. As far as the various parameters are concerned, we assume α, β, γ, δ, and $k \geq 0$. A zero value of k would imply a very large pollution cost when the two firms locate close to each other. An increase in k typically decreases the pollution cost ceteris paribus, while δ has an opposite effect on the cost of pollution as long as $(k + x_B - x_A) < 1$.

Transportation Cost

Consumers located along the market incur a cost when they travel to the site of the firm to buy its product (the difference between mill price and delivered price). Since this cost of transportation induces consumers to buy from the closest firm, a consumer located at a point half way between x_A and x_B will be indifferent between the firms for any given transportation cost of c per unit of distance. So the firm located at x_A will serve all the consumers to its left, and those located to its right up to the half way point between itself and the firm at x_B $\left(q_A = \frac{x_A + x_B}{2}\right)$. The firm at x_B will then serve the rest of the market and $q_B = 1 - q_A$. The transportation cost per unit for each consumer is 'c' multiplied by the distance between the consumer and the nearest firm (x). The total transportation cost for all the consumers located along the market is obtained by integrating the product of c and x over the length of the market.

$$TC = \int_0^{x_A} cxdx + \int_0^{\left(\frac{x_B+x_A}{2}\right)-(x_A)} cxdx + \int_0^{(x_B)-\left(\frac{x_B+x_A}{2}\right)} cxdx + \int_0^{1-x_B} cxdx$$

$$= \frac{cx_A^2}{2} + \frac{c(x_B - x_A)^2}{4} + \frac{c(1-x_B)^2}{2}$$

Since the firms have no marginal production costs, the total social cost is the sum of the transportation costs incurred by the consumers and the pollution cost borne by the downstream producer.

Liability Rules

A policy option available to deal with externalities is to use different liability rules. This policy option becomes important when negotiation between the affected parties is not practical. Liability rules become more important in cases like polluted rivers where it is hard to define property rights over the use of this resource. The rule determines whether or not the polluter is liable to compensate the victims of its pollution. Our model incorporates two types of liability rules:

No Liability: When the polluting firm is *not liable* to compensate the victim of the externality it generates, and the fixed price the firms charge is p, the profit of the upstream firm is

$$\pi_A = p\, q_A, \text{ and}$$

$$\pi_B = p\, q_B - \gamma \frac{q_A^{\alpha} q_B^{\beta}}{(k + x_B - x_A)^{\delta}}$$

Full Liability : When the polluting firm is *liable* to compensate the victim of its pollution, and the fixed price charged by the firms is p, the profit of the upstream firm is

$$\pi_A = p\, q_A - \gamma \frac{q_A^{\alpha} q_B^{\beta}}{(k + x_B - x_A)^{\delta}} \text{ and}$$

$\pi_B = p\, q_B$ is the profit of the downstream firm.

Optimal Locations

In the absence of externalities, the socially optimal locations for the two firms would be at the first and third quartiles. These locations would minimize transportation costs incurred by the consumers. In the presence of externalities (in this case pollution) which decrease with distance, the pollution cost will be least when the firms locate at the extremes of the market. The social cost minimizing locations of the firms would therefore depend on the magnitudes of the transportation cost and the pollution cost. If the transportation cost is very large, the socially optimal positions of the firms would be closer to the first and third quartiles. When the pollution cost is very high, it would be more beneficial to society if the firms located close to the two ends of the market. Thus, the socially optimal locations may lead to maximal differentiation.

Duopolistic Interaction

Sequential Location

The firms enter the market in the sophisticated manner described by Prescott and Visscher (1977). Since relocation in product space may involve high costs of retooling, advertising and moving plant sites, firms can be thought of as making "once-for-all profit-maximizing location decisions" one at a time. This model incorporates the idea put forth by these authors in a more narrow sense: when the product characteristic being considered is the location of the firm. The model also takes into account the firms' awareness that their decisions are relatively permanent and their ability to correctly anticipate the decisions of firms that will follow them. Each firm is thus aware of where the other will locate and the profits that will accrue to both of them as a result of the locations. The model does not allow the firms to locate at the same place, i.e., they cannot locate on top of each other.

Discrete Examples Illustrating the Interaction

Suppose the firms are restricted to locate at the following points in and outside the market (-0.25, 0, 0.25, 0.5, 0.75, 1, 1.25). Table 1 A shows the profits for the second firm for different locations of the first firm and the preferred location of the second firm for each location of the first firm. For example, when the first firm locates at the first quartile (x_1 = 0.25), the second firm earns the highest profit when it locates at the center (x_2 = 0.5) of the market. The second to last column in the table shows the preferred locations for the second firm, and the last column shows the first firm's profits corresponding to these locations of the second firm. Since its profit is highest when the second firm locates at the center of the market, the first firm will choose to locate at the first quartile in a regime where the polluting firm is not liable for the damages it imposes on others.

Table 1 A Profits and location choice of firm 2 in a no-liability situation when $\gamma = 0.857$, $k = 0.286$ and $\alpha = \beta = \delta = p = 1$.

x_2 / x_1	-.25	0	.25	.5	.75	1	1.25	x_2^*	π_1
-.25	-	1.000	1.000	0.785	0.625	0.494	0.380	0.250	0
0	0	-	0.700	0.546	0.431	0.333	0.244	0.250	0.125
.25	0	0.125	-	0.250	0.227	0.181	0.125	0.500	0.375
.5	0.125	0.250	0.375	-	0	0.046	0.035	0.250	0.250
.75	0.250	0.375	0.500	0.625	-	-0.050	0	0.500	0
1	0.375	0.500	0.625	0.750	0.875	-	0	0.750	-0.050
1.25	0.500	0.625	0.750	0.875	1.000	1.000	-	1.000	0

Table 1B shows the location choice for the two firms in a full-liability situation. The first firm earns the highest profit when it locates at the third quartile ($x_1 = 0.75$) and the second firm locates at the center of the market ($x_2 = 0.5$).

Table 1 B Profits and location choice of firm 2 in a full-liability situation when $\gamma = 0.857$, $k = 0.286$ and $\alpha = \beta = \delta = p = 1$.

x_2 / x_1	-.25	0	.25	.5	.75	1	1.25	x_2^*	π_1
-.25	-	1.000	0.750	0.500	0.250	0	0.500	0.250	0
0	0	-	0.875	0.750	0.625	0.500	0.375	0.250	-0.050
.25	0	-0.050	-	0.625	0.500	0.375	0.250	0.500	0
.5	0.035	0.046	0	-	0.375	0.25	0.125	0.750	0.250
.75	0.125	0.181	0.227	0.250	-	0.125	0	0.500	0.375
1	0.244	0.333	0.431	0.546	0.700	-	0	0.750	0.125
1.25	0.380	0.494	0.625	0.750	1.000	1.000	-	1.000	0

Continuous Location Choice

Suppose the firms are no longer restricted to locate at discrete points in the market, and are allowed a continuous location choice. When there is a no-liability rule in force, the first firm to enter the market may choose to locate such that the second firm might be indifferent between locating just upstream of the first firm so that $x_{2A} = x_1 - \varepsilon$ and locating at a downstream position, x_{2B}, in terms of maximizing profits. So the first firm will locate so as to assure that

$$\pi_{2A} = \pi_{2B}$$

when $\pi_{2A} = px_{2A}$ (or px_A with $x_1 = x_B$)

$$\text{and } \pi_{2B} = max \left\{ p\left(1 - \frac{x_B + x_A}{2}\right) - \frac{\gamma\left(\frac{x_B + x_A}{2}\right)^{\alpha}\left(1 - \frac{x_B + x_A}{2}\right)^{\beta}}{(k + x_B - x_A)^{\delta}} \right\}$$

with $x_1 = x_A$

The second firm will experience increasing profits as it locates closer to the first firm on its left (Fig. 1a). It earns the maximum profit when it locates right next to the first firm. On the downstream side of the first firm, the second firm's profits increase with the distance between the firms at first. After a point, the profits decrease because it has to share more of the market with its rival. When the polluting or upstream firm is not liable to compensate the downstream firm for its clean up costs, the second firm will be indifferent between locating just to the left of the first firm and downstream at point A in terms of the profits it earns.

Figures 1c and 1e illustrate non-optimal location choices of the first firm. When the first firm locates more upstream (as compared to the case shown in Fig. 1a), the second firm clearly benefits from choosing a downstream location. On the other hand, the second firm would earn much higher profits if it located upstream of the first firm (Fig. 1e) when the first firm selects a relatively downstream location.

In a full-liability scenario, the second firm to enter the market may choose to locate just to the right of the first firm so that $x_{2B} = x_1 + \varepsilon$ or at a point upstream x_{2A} where it can earn the same level of profits as it would earn downstream. So the first firm will locate so as to assure that

$$\pi_{2A} = \pi_{2B}$$

$$\text{when } \pi_{2A} = max \left\{ p\left(\frac{x_B + x_A}{2}\right) - \frac{\gamma\left(\frac{x_B + x_A}{2}\right)^{\alpha}\left(1 - \frac{x_B + x_A}{2}\right)^{\beta}}{(k + x_B - x_A)^{\delta}} \right\}$$

with $x_1 = x_B$

and $\pi_{2B} = p\ (1 - x_B)$ with $x_1 = x_A$.

When the polluting firm has to compensate the victim of its pollution, the second firm experiences a decline in profits as it moves away from the first firm (located at x1 in Fig. 1b) towards the downstream end of the market. If it chooses to locate to the left (upstream) of the first firm, its profits increase at first and then decrease as it locates closer to its rival. As the distance between the firms decreases, the cost of pollution that the second firm (now upstream) has to bear increases. The second firm will be indifferent between locating just to the right of the first firm and at point A since it will earn maximum profits at both these points.

Figures 1d and 1f exhibit non-optimal location choices of the first firm. In Fig. 1d, the second firm earns much higher profits when it locates to the right of the first firm. The opposite case is shown in Fig. 1f, where the second firm would prefer an upstream location.

The location decision of the firms is affected by the different values taken on by the parameters in the pollution cost function. The next section elaborates the effect these parameters have on the location and profits of the firms, the magnitude of the pollution externality generated and the transportation costs borne by consumers under the different liability rules. The comparative statics are performed for three cases:

i. when the pollution cost is proportional to the output of both firms ($\alpha = \beta = 1$)

ii. when the pollution cost is proportional to the output of the upstream firm ($\alpha = 1, \beta = 0$) and

iii. when the pollution cost is proportional to the output of the downstream firm ($\alpha = 0, \beta = 1$)

The following sections discuss the first case in detail and present the important results obtained from the other two cases.

Comparative Statics

Case I: Pollution cost is proportional to the output of both firms ($\alpha = \beta = 1$)

As seen in tables 2a-2l, under both liability scenarios, the distance between the firms increases with an increase in the intensity of pollution and as δ increases. In geographic space this could imply higher transportation costs for consumers for certain combinations of the parameter values. This could also mean greater product differentiation. k has an opposite effect on the distance between the firms, making them cluster in the center of the market when it takes on high values.

The pollution cost under both liability rules increases with γ and k and generally decreases with δ. Higher k values result in higher pollution cost because they make the firms locate closer to each other. The cost this pollution externality imposes on society is the sum of the pollution cost and transportation cost. This total social cost increases with an increase in k for certain parameter values.

The effect of the parameters k, γ and δ on the profits of the firms is opposite under the two liability rules. When a no-liability rule is in force, the profit of the downstream firm increases with k and decreases with γ and δ ceteris paribus. The upstream firm's profit increases with δ, decreases with k and can increase, decrease or remain constant with γ depending on what values the other parameters take on. In a full-liability regime, the profit of the upstream firm increases with k and decreases with γ and δ ceteris paribus. The downstream firm's profit increases with δ, decreases with k and can increase, decrease or remain constant with γ depending on what values the other parameters take on.

Observations

(1) The results of the simulations indicate that in the presence of pollution externalities, for certain combinations of parameter values there is evidence of too much or too little geographic differentiation (product differentiation) in this Hotelling-type market.

(2) The different cases show that the liability rules create different incentives for the firms to change their production (polluting) technologies. In Case I, the polluting firm prefers the no-liability rule while the victim of the pollution prefers to be compensated for the damages imposed upon it. If a full-liability rule is in force, the upstream firm would have an incentive to adopt a less-polluting technology. This incentive becomes stronger in Case II where the polluting firm loses profits as the pollution intensity increases under both liability rules. In Case III, both firms face declining profits in the face of increasing pollution intensity when there is full-liability and would thus be inclined to adopt a less-polluting technology.

(3) The pollution cost associated with different levels of pollution intensity are the highest in Case II, under the no-liability scenario. This case also exhibits the highest levels of total social cost. Under the full-liability scenario, the highest pollution costs and corresponding total costs are observed in Case III. In the no-liability scenario, the most differentiation for a particular level of pollution intensity is observed in Case III, while Case II exhibits this when there is full liability. These observations point to an interesting symmetry between the different liability scenarios in the three cases considered.

(4) In Case I, the distance between the firms and the pollution and transportation costs remain the same under the two liability scenarios for different values of the parameters. The profits of the upstream and the downstream firms get interchanged when the liability rule changes. A similar symmetry is observed between the no-liability scenario of Case II and the full-liability scenario of Case III and the full-liability scenario of Case II and the no-liability scenario of Case III.

(5) In certain situations when the second firm locates just to the left or right of the first firm there are very high pollution costs, and when it decides to locate very far upstream or downstream, the cost of transportation goes up. Therefore there exists a tradeoff between these two costs. Since firms are not expected to let their actions be guided by welfare considerations that entail minimizing costs to society, the role of social planners becomes important. Planners can adopt measures that would enable this minimum social cost situation.

Policy Options

Some policy options available to planners are internalization of the externality, liability rules, taxes, and site regulation which could take the form of large-lot zoning or actual physical separation of the economic agents (non-conforming land uses).

Internalizing the externality involves putting both firms under the same ownership, so that the amount of waste discharged into the river would be that which maximizes joint profits.

Internalization after entry by one or both firms will not necessarily result in the optimal location of the firms. In this process, the output level of one of the firms would have to be reduced to zero. However, to deter entry by another firm, the inactive firm would either have to be kept operational or the management would have to buy two licenses from the entry-regulating authority. If the firm located closer to the center of the market serves all the customers, the transportation costs would be reduced. This could however, lead to the minimum social cost implied by symmetry only for certain coefficients of the transportation and pollution costs (Gupt and Veendorp; 1997 a, b).

The results of the simulation show that the optimal location choice of the firms for different combinations of the parameters α, β, δ, γ and k does not always coincide with the social optimum under the different liability rules.

Another option available to planners is that of taxation. In the continuous location example, a per unit tax imposed before the firms locate in the market increases the distance between the firms. As a result, the pollution cost imposed on the downstream firm is smaller as compared to the no-tax situation. However the magnitude of the "externality" imposed on the consumers in the form of transportation costs increases. As the tax rate increases, the pollution cost decreases for different levels of pollution intensity and the transportation cost increases. For lower values of the tax, the decrease in the pollution cost is of the order of a few percentage points, and there is a small or no change in the transportation cost. The resulting total social cost is lower compared to the no-tax situation. For higher tax rates, the pollution cost decreases by a considerable amount, but the corresponding transportation cost is much higher. This trade-off between the decreasing pollution cost and the increasing transportation cost can give rise to conflict between different interest groups. In order to reduce pollution costs by an appreciable amount, a higher tax rate must be imposed on the polluter. This tax rate will in turn make the firms locate further away from each other and force consumers to pay higher transportation costs.

A comparison of the effect of liability rules and taxes on firm profits reveals that, the polluting firm prefers a liability rule over a tax only when the tax rate is very high and k is equal to zero. The victim of its pollution, prefers to be compensated irrespective of the rate of tax and the value k takes on. For very low tax rates, and non-zero values of k, the polluting firm prefers to pay a tax.

Another policy option is that of zoning (which would involve physically separating the economic agents). The most commonly used rationale behind the use of this instrument is the need to separate non conforming land uses in the presence of externalities. In this case, through its effect on the location of the firms, the externality can cause non convexities in the social cost set. This would imply a local minimum instead of a global one. Baumol and Oates (1988) suggest that physically separating the economic agents that generate the externality and those that suffer on account of it may be the best option to minimize the total social costs associated with the externality.

Conclusion

(1) In this Hotelling-type market with externalities, the first firm to enter the market prefers to locate upstream in a no-liability scenario and downstream when there is a full-liability rule in force.

(2) Liability rules create different incentives for the firms to change their production technologies depending on which firm's output affects the pollution cost. The social and pollution costs are highest when the pollution cost is affected by the output levels of both firms in a no-liability scenario. In this scenario the firms have no incentive to adopt cleaner technologies. When the polluting firm is liable to pay damages, it loses profits with increasing pollution intensity and has an incentive to "clean up."

(3) The simulation of the firms' location decisions in the presence of an externality shows non-optimal locations from the society's point of view for different combinations of the parameter values. Non-optimal locations imply higher social costs. Planners can use different tools to minimize these costs. Internalization of the externality and liability rules do not always result in socially optimal minimum cost locations. A per unit tax imposed prior to location also does not lead to optimal location. For certain combinations of the parameter values, physically separating the firms through site regulation or zoning may be the most appropriate policy option.

References

Baumol, William J. and Wallace E. Oates (1988). *Theory of Environmental Policy. Second Edition*. Cambridge, England: Cambridge University Press.

Chiang, Alpha C. (1984), *Fundamental Methods of Mathematical Economics. Third Edition*. Singapore: McGraw-Hill Book Company.

Coase, Ronald. (1960), The Problem of Social Cost. *Journal of Law and Economics*, 1-44.

D' Aspremont, C., J, Jaskold-Gabszewicz and J. F. Thisse. (1979), On Hotelling's Stability in Competition. *Econometrica*, 47(5), 1145-1150.

Eaton, B.C. and R. Lipsey (1975), The Principle of Minimum Differentiation Reconsidered: Some New Developments in the Theory of Spatial Competition. *Review of Economic Studies*, 42, 27-50.

Gabszewicz, J. Jaskold and J.-F. Thisse (1986), On the Nature of Competition With Differentiated Products. *The Economic Journal*, 96, 160-172.

Germain, M. (1989), Externalitiés, Taxation et Traitement de la Pollution dans le Cadre d'un Duopole de Cournot. *Recherches Economiques de Louvain*, 60, 273-92.

Gupt, Yamini and E.C.H. Veendorp (1997a), Externalities in a Hotelling Model. *Southern Economic Journal*, 64 (1), 321-325.

– – (1997b), Competition in a Linear Market with Externalities. Published in proceedings of the 3rd International Interdisciplinary Conference on the Environment (June 1997), Cambridge, MA.

Hotelling, H. (1929), Stability in Competition. *The Economic Journal*, 39, 41-57.

Kamien, M.I., N.L. Schwartz, and F.T. Dolbear (1966), Asymmetry Between Bribes and Charges, *Water Resources Research*, 2, 147-157.

Kneese, A.V. (1964), *The Economics of Regional Water Quality Management*. Baltimore, MD: Johns Hopkins Press.

Kneese, A.V. and B.T. Bower (1968), *Managing Water Quality: Economics, Technology, Institutions*. Baltimore, MD: Johns Hopkins Press.

Levin, D. (1985). Taxation Within Cournot Oligopoly, *Journal of Public Economics*, 27, 281-290.

Marchand, J.R. and K.P Russell (1973), Externalities, Liability, Separability, and Resource Allocation. *American Economic Review*, 63, 611-620.

Nutter, W.G. (1968), The Coase Theorem on Social Cost: A Footnote, *Journal of Law and Economics*, 11, 503-507.

Ortolano, L. (1984), *Environmental Planning and Decision Making*. New York: John Wiley and Sons.

Pigou, A. C. (1920), *The Economics of Welfare*. London: MacMillan and Co., Ltd.

Prescott, E.C. and M. Visscher (1977) Sequential Location Among Firms With Foresight, *Bell Journal of Economics and Management Science*, 8, 378-393.

Tabuchi, T. and J.F. Thisse (1995) Asymmetric Equilibria in Spatial Competition. *International Journal of Industrial Organization*, 13(2), 213-227.

Thomann, R. V. (1972), *Systems Analysis and Water Quality Management*. New York: Environmental Research and Applications, Inc. (reissued by McGraw Hill, New York).

Tybout, R.A. (1972), Pricing Pollution and Other Negative Externalities. *Bell Journal Of Economics and Management Science*, 3, 252-266.

Veendotp, E.C.H. and A. Zambaras (1992). Externalities in Oligopolistic Markets. Clark University Discussion Paper.

Wellisz, S. (1964), On External Diseconomies and the Government-Assisted Invisible Hand. *Economica*, 31, 345-362.

Figure 1a: The location options available to the second firm and its corresponding profit levels when the first firm locates at x1 in a no-liability scenario. $\alpha = \beta = \delta = p = 1$, $k = 0.2$ and $\gamma = 0.5$

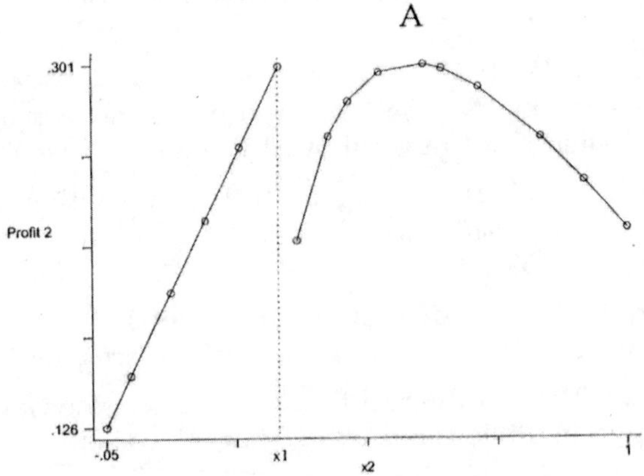

Figure 1b: The location options available to the second firm and its corresponding profit levels when the first firm locates at x1 in a full-liability scenario. $\alpha = \beta = \delta = p = 1$, $k = 0.2$ and $\gamma = 0.5$

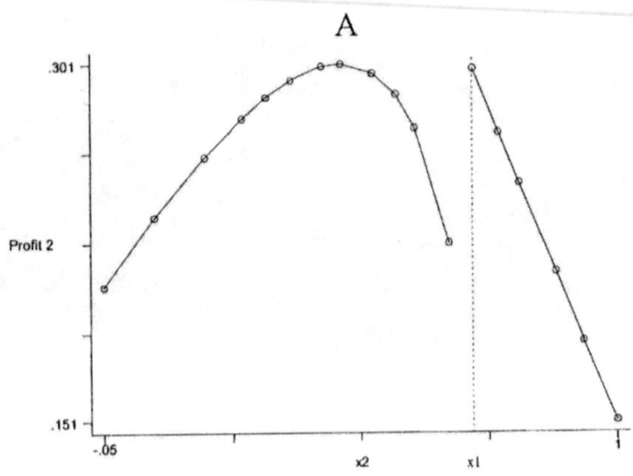

Figure 1c: When the first firm does not locate at a point such that the second can be indifferent between locating upstream or downstream in a no-liability scenario. $\alpha = \beta = \delta = p = 1$, $k = 0.2$ and $\gamma = 0.5$

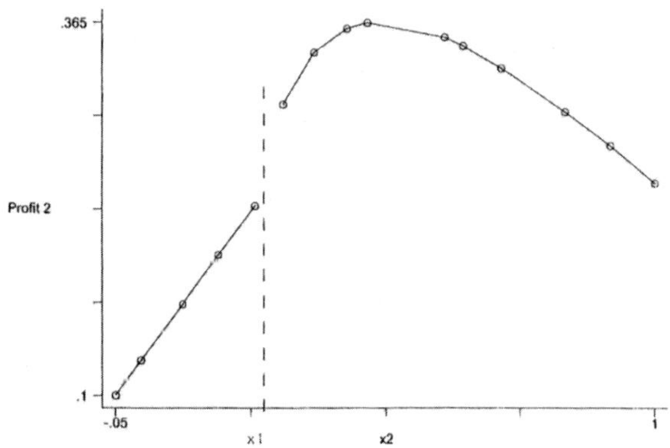

Figure 1d: When the first firm does not locate at a point such that the second can be indifferent between locating upstream or downstream in a full-liability scenario. $\alpha = \beta = \delta = p = 1$, $k = 0.2$ and $\gamma = 0.5$

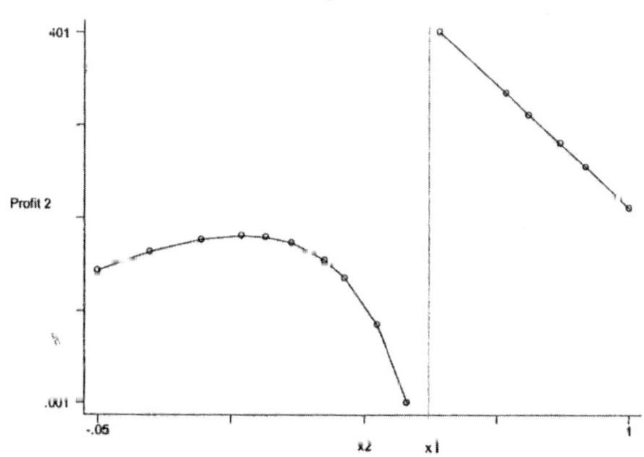

Figure 1e: When the first firm does not locate at a point such that the second can be indifferent between locating upstream or downstream in a no-liability scenario. $\alpha = \beta = \delta = p = 1$, k = 0.2 and $\gamma = 0.5$

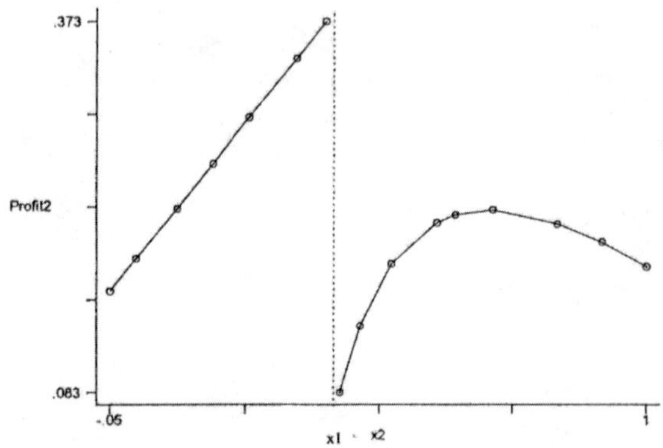

Figure 1f: When the first firm does not locate at a point such that the second can be indifferent between locating upstream or downstream in a full-liability scenario. $\alpha = \beta = \delta = p = 1$, k = 0.2 and $\gamma = 0.5$

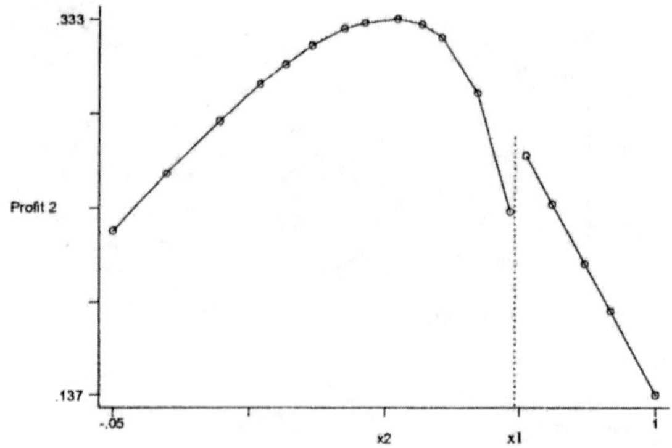

Table 2a The profits, pollution, and transportation costs associated with the firms in a no-liability situation when $\alpha = 1, \beta = 1, \delta = 1, p = 1$ and $k = 0$

γ	x_{2A} upstream	x_{2B} downstream	$x_{2B} - x_{2A}$	TC	PC	π_1 profit of upstream firm	π_2 profit of downstream firm
0.1	0.388	0.612	0.224	0.163	0.112	0.500	0.388
0.2	0.342	0.658	0.316	0.142	0.158	0.500	0.342
0.3	0.306	0.694	0.388	0.131	0.194	0.500	0.306
0.4	0.276	0.724	0.448	0.126	0.224	0.500	0.276
0.5	0.250	0.750	0.500	0.125	0.250	0.500	0.250
0.6	0.226	0.774	0.548	0.126	0.274	0.500	0.226
0.7	0.204	0.796	0.592	0.129	0.296	0.500	0.204

TC is the transportation cost

PC is the pollution cost

Table 2b The profits, pollution, and transportation costs associated with the firms in a no-liability situation when $\alpha = 1, \beta = 1, \delta = 1, p = 1$ and $k = 0.2$

γ	x_{2A} upstream	x_{2B} downstream	$x_{2B} - x_{2A}$	TC	PC	π_1 profit of upstream firm	π_2 profit of downstream firm
0.1	0.439	0.456	0.017	0.244	0.114	0.447	0.439
0.2	0.393	0.496	0.103	0.207	0.163	0.444	0.393
0.3	0.357	0.525	0.168	0.184	0.201	0.441	0.357
0.4	0.328	0.547	0.219	0.168	0.235	0.438	0.328
0.5	0.302	0.565	0.263	0.158	0.265	0.433	0.302
0.6	0.278	0.579	0.301	0.150	0.293	0.429	0.278
0.7	0.256	0.590	0.334	0.145	0.320	0.423	0.256

Table 2c The profits, pollution, and transportation costs associated with the firms in a no-liability situation when $\alpha = 1, \beta = 1, \delta = 1,\ p = 1$ and $\gamma = 0.5$

k	x_{2A} upstream	x_{2B} downs-tream	$x_{2B} - x_{2A}$	TC	PC	π_1 profit of upstream firm	π_2 profit of downs tream firm
0	0.250	0.750	0.500	0.125	0.250	0.500	0.250
0.1	0.275	0.658	0.383	0.133	0.258	0.467	0.275
0.2	0.302	0.565	0.263	0.158	0.265	0.433	0.302
0.3	0.329	0.471	0.142	0.199	0.271	0.400	0.329

Table 2d The profits, pollution, and transportation costs associated with the firms in a no-liability situation when $\alpha = 1, \beta = 1, \delta = 2,\ p = 1$ and $k = 0$

γ	x_{2A} upstream	x_{2B} downs-tream	$x_{2B} - x_{2A}$	TC	PC	π_1 profit of upstream firm	π_2 profit of downs tream firm
0.1	0.327	0.798	0.471	0.129	0.111	0.562	0.327
0.2	0.282	0.881	0.599	0.137	0.136	0.582	0.282
0.3	0.252	0.942	0.690	0.152	0.152	0.597	0.252
0.4	0.227	0.993	0.766	0.172	0.163	0.610	0.227
0.5	0.207	1.037	0.830	0.194	0.171	0.622	0.207
0.6	0.190	1.077	0.887	0.218	0.177	0.634	0.190
0.7	0.174	1.115	0.941	0.243	0.181	0.644	0.174

Table 2e The profits, pollution, and transportation costs associated with the firms in a no-liability situation when $\alpha = 1, \beta = 1, \delta = 2$, $p = 1$ and $k = 0.2$

γ	x_{2A} upstream	x_{2B} downs-tream	$x_{2B} - x_{2A}$	TC	PC	π_1 profit of upstream firm	π_2 profit of downs tream firm
0.1	0.376	0.641	0.265	0.153	0.115	0.509	0.376
0.2	0.331	0.721	0.390	0.132	0.143	0.526	0.331
0.3	0.299	0.779	0.480	0.127	0.161	0.539	0.299
0.4	0.274	0.827	0.553	0.129	0.175	0.551	0.274
0.5	0.254	0.869	0.615	0.135	0.185	0.561	0.254
0.6	0.235	0.907	0.672	0.145	0.193	0.571	0.235
0.7	0.219	0.942	0.723	0.156	0.200	0.581	0.219

Table 2f The profits, pollution, and transportation costs associated with the firms in a no-liability situation when $\alpha = 1, \beta = 1, \delta = 2$, $p = 1$ and $\gamma = 0.5$

k	x_{2A} upstream	x_{2B} downs-tream	$x_{2B} - x_{2A}$	TC	PC	π_1 profit of upstream firm	π_2 profit of downs tream firm
0	0.207	1 037	0.030	0.194	0.171	0.622	0.207
0.1	0.230	0.954	0.724	0.159	0.178	0.592	0.230
0.2	0.254	0.869	0.615	0.135	0.185	0.561	0.254
0.3	0.277	0.783	0.506	0.126	0.192	0.530	0.278

Table 2g The profits, pollution, and transportation costs associated with the firms in a full-liability situation when $\alpha = 1, \beta = 1, \delta = 1,\ p = 1$ and $k = 0$

γ	x_{2A} upstream	x_{2B} downs-tream	$x_{2B} - x_{2A}$	TC	PC	π_1 profit of upstream firm	π_2 profit of downs tream firm
0.1	0.388	0.612	0.224	0.163	0.112	0.388	0.500
0.2	0.342	0.658	0.316	0.142	0.158	0.342	0.500
0.3	0.306	0.694	0.388	0.131	0.194	0.306	0.500
0.4	0.276	0.724	0.448	0.126	0.224	0.276	0.500
0.5	0.250	0.750	0.500	0.125	0.25	0.25	0.500
0.6	0.226	0.774	0.548	0.126	0.274	0.226	0.500
0.7	0.204	0.796	0.592	0.129	0.296	0.204	0.500

Table 2h The profits, pollution, and transportation costs associated with the firms in a full-liability situation when $\alpha = 1, \beta = 1, \delta = 1,\ p = 1$ and $k = 0.2$

γ	x_{2A} upstream	x_{2B} downs-tream	$x_{2B} - x_{2A}$	TC	PC	π_1 profit of upstream firm	π_2 profit of downs tream firm
0.1	0.544	0.561	0.017	0.244	0.114	0.439	0.447
0.2	0.504	0.607	0.103	0.207	0.163	0.393	0.444
0.3	0.475	0.643	0.168	0.184	0.201	0.357	0.441
0.4	0.453	0.672	0.219	0.168	0.235	0.328	0.438
0.5	0.435	0.698	0.263	0.158	0.265	0.302	0.433
0.6	0.421	0.722	0.301	0.150	0.293	0.278	0.429
0.7	0.410	0.744	0.334	0.145	0.320	0.256	0.423

Table 2i The profits, pollution, and transportation costs associated with the firms in a full-liability situation when $\alpha = 1, \beta = 1, \delta = 1, p = 1$ and $\gamma = 0.5$

k	x_{2A} upstream	x_{2B} downstream	$x_{2B} - x_{2A}$	TC	PC	π_1 profit of upstream firm	π_2 profit of downstream firm
0	0.250	0.750	0.500	0.125	0.250	0.250	0.500
0.1	0.342	0.725	0.383	0.133	0.258	0.275	0.467
0.2	0.435	0.698	0.263	0.158	0.265	0.302	0.433
0.3	0.529	0.671	0.142	0.199	0.271	0.329	0.400

Table 2j The profits, pollution, and transportation costs associated with the firms in a full-liability situation when $\alpha = 1, \beta = 1, \delta = 2, p = 1$ and $k = 0$

γ	x_{2A} upstream	x_{2B} downstream	$x_{2B} - x_{2A}$	TC	PC	π_1 profit of upstream firm	π_2 profit of downstream firm
0.1	0.203	0.673	0.470	0.129	0.111	0.327	0.562
0.2	0.119	0.718	0.599	0.137	0.136	0.282	0.582
0.3	0.058	0.748	0.690	0.152	0.152	0.252	0.597
0.4	0.007	0.773	0.766	0.172	0.163	0.227	0.610
0.5	-0.037	0.793	0.830	0.194	0.171	0.207	0.622
0.6	-0.077	0.810	0.887	0.218	0.177	0.190	0.634
0.7	-0.115	0.826	0.941	0.243	0.181	0.174	0.644

Table 2k The profits, pollution, and transportation costs associated with the firms in a full-liability situation when $\alpha = 1, \beta = 1, \delta = 2, p = 1$ and $k = 0.2$

γ	x_{2A} upstream	x_{2B} downstream	$x_{2B} - x_{2A}$	TC	PC	π_1 profit of upstream firm	π_2 profit of downstream firm
0.1	0.359	0.624	0.265	0.153	0.115	0.376	0.509
0.2	0.279	0.669	0.390	0.132	0.143	0.331	0.526
0.3	0.221	0.701	0.480	0.127	0.161	0.299	0.539
0.4	0.173	0.726	0.553	0.129	0.175	0.274	0.551
0.5	0.131	0.746	0.615	0.135	0.185	0.254	0.561
0.6	0.093	0.765	0.672	0.145	0.193	0.235	0.571
0.7	0.058	0.781	0.723	0.156	0.200	0.219	0.581

Table 2l The profits, pollution, and transportation costs associated with the firms in a full-liability situation when $\alpha = 1, \beta = 1, \delta = 2, p = 1$ and $\gamma = 0.5$

k	x_{2A} upstream	x_{2B} downstream	$x_{2B} - x_{2A}$	TC	PC	π_1 profit of upstream firm	π_2 profit of downstream firm
0	-0.037	0.793	0.830	0.194	0.171	0.207	0.622
0.1	0.046	0.770	0.724	0.159	0.178	0.230	0.592
0.2	0.131	0.746	0.615	0.135	0.185	0.254	0.561
0.3	0.217	0.722	0.505	0.126	0.192	0.278	0.530

Economic Valuation of Wetlands: Problems and Prospects

14

Amit Love, Shvetank Sharma, Radhey Shyam Sharma, C.R. Babu

Introduction

Natural resource accounting is an economic instrument for achieving sustainable development. Understanding of the ecological processes that regulate ecosystem functions is central to economic valuation of natural resources. Economic valuation of natural resources requires efficient methodologies to capture the values derived from ecosystem functions. The wetland ecosystems are the most productive ecosystems in the biosphere and are increasingly being threatened due to developmental activities. Economic valuation of these ecosystems may yield strategies that promote their sustainable utilization. Problems and prospects of economic valuation of wetlands are highlighted in the paper, which is split into three parts.

Part one gives an idea of ecosystems with particular focus on Wetland ecosystems. Part two discusses issues related to the economic valuation of wetlands. The last part brings together the conclusions of the study.

Wetland Ecosystems

Ecosystems

Natural ecosystems provide a number of ecosystem services, which are critical for the survival and development of human society. These services are generated due to ecosystem processes which occur through interactions between biotic and abiotic components and between different biota of the ecosystems. The choices we exercise on how we utilize natural ecosystems determines the maintenance and sustainability of the ecosystem services leading to sustainable development.

To sustainably utilize natural ecosystems so as to maintain the flow of goods and services, efficient management of ecosystems is a must. Management of natural ecosystems is particularly problematic due their extremely complex non-linear character with extensive interconnections among the components. Moreover, ecosystems exist in different states on a spatio-temporal scale that lead to qualitative and quantitative shifts in the generation of goods and services. Ecosystems generate these services on a sustainable basis only when they function within their natural threshold limits. Certain key ecological processes and keystone species determine threshold limits of an ecosystem. Therefore to sustainably utilize ecosystem resources it is necessary that the role of these key ecological processes and keystone species is made explicit and quantified.

Due to poorly understood nature of ecosystems, and hidden nature of ecosystem services, natural ecosystems undergo rapid degradation. The importance of ecosystem services is widely appreciated only upon their loss. In other words, ecosystems are natural capital assets which require appropriate management if they are to produce a sustainable flow of income. The management process requires use of investible funds, which otherwise could have been used for alternative purposes. It is therefore essential to undertake economic valuation of ecosystem resources not only for the conservation of natural ecosystems but also for achieving sustainable development. The complexities involved in ecosystem valuation, scope and limitation of ecosystem valuation can be understood more clearly using the example of wetland ecosystems.

Definition, Characteristics and Kinds of Wetland Ecosystems

Wetland ecosystems are among the most productive ecosystem in the world, which not only support unique flora and fauna, but also provide ecosystem services beneficial to the human society. Wetlands encompass a wide range of habitats from areas under water to seasonally inundated, predominantly dry areas, like floodplains. Heterogeneity in wetland habitats due to variation in geomorphology, hydrology and vegetation type has led to difficulty in correct identification and delimitation of wetland ecosystems. The World Conservation Union (IUCN) adopted a formal internationally acceptable definition of wetlands in the Ramsar Convention. According to the Ramsar convention wetland are defined as: "areas of marsh, fen, peatland or water, wether natural or artificial, permanent or temporary, with water that is static or flowing, fresh, brackish or salt, including areas of marine water, the depth of which at low tide does not exceed six metres." The rationale for such broad definition of wetlands stemmed from the desire to embrace all kinds of wetlands ecosystems. Wetland ecosystems spread across the world account for about 6% of the global land area (Turner, 1991).

Wetlands can be classified into 5 broad categories: (i) estuarine ecosystem; (ii) marine ecosystem; (iii) riverine ecosystem; (iv) palustrine ecosystems; (v) lacustrine ecosystems. Estuarine ecosystems are those areas where rivers meet the sea and the salinity is intermediate between salt and freshwater; these areas are exemplified by deltas, mud flats and salt marshes. Marine ecosystems are those areas which are not influenced by river flows and are represented by shorelines and coral reefs. Riverine ecosystems are those areas that are periodically inundated by river overtopping and include water meadows, floodplains and oxbow lakes. Palustrine ecosystems are predominantly covered by water and these ecosystems include marshes and fen. Lacustrine ecosystems are permanently submerged with water and there is little or no surface flow and are exemplified by ponds and lakes.

Functions and Benefits of Wetlands

Human societies living near the wetland ecosystems sustain their livelihoods predominantly based upon the resources of wetland ecosystems. Fish is a major source of dietary protein not only for the communities living near the wetlands but also for communities further inland. The seasonal grazing lands provide fodder for the livestock of local communities. Tree species dispersed through the wetland ecosystems provide fuelwood to the local people. Certain wetland ecosystems have nutrient rich, high moisture containing soils (floodplains) which support dry season agriculture. The surface and ground water which is present in the wetland ecosystems is a major source of not water only for drinking purposes but can also be used for practicing agriculture and in industries if used sustainably. Besides these direct benefits derived form the structural components (land, air and living organisms) of wetlands, the ecological functions provide intangible ecosystem services. These intangible services include: (i) biogeochemical cycling and nutrient retention, (ii) ground water recharge, (iii) bioremediation, (iv) flood mitigation, (v) storm protection and (vi) sediment trapping. Wetland ecosystems being transition zone between aquatic and terrestrial ecosystems support and sustain a large diversity of flora and fauna. In short, wetlands are valuable multiple use economic resource which are critical for the development of sustainable economies.

Status of Wetlands

Wetland ecosystems are among the most threatened of all environmental resources which are rapidly diminishing due to anthropogenic activities. During last 100 years US has lost around 47% of its wetland, whereas UK and New Zealand had lost around 60% and 90% of their wetlands respectively (WCMC, 1992). For most of nations of South Asia the loss of wetland has been estimated to the tune of 80% (UNEP, 1992).

The over utilization of total wetlands stock has been the result of a combined effect of economic development pressures, information failure, market failure and intervention failure (Turner, 1991). Conversion of wetlands for alternative uses is largely due to information failure i.e. policy makers and planners are unaware of the goods and services which are provided by the wetlands. Moreover, due to market failure majority of these goods and services are not traded in conventional market economy and therefore no economic values are assigned to them. Information and market failures lead to intervention failure i.e. inefficient policies are made by the planners with regards to conservation of wetland ecosystems. Wetlands being multiple-use economic resource, which are undergoing rapid degradation, it is necessary that their goods and services are made explicit and economic values assigned using suitable economic valuation techniques. This would lead to more rationale decision being taken with regards to conservation of wetlands and their sustainable utilization based upon the economic efficiency criteria.

Economic Valuation of Wetlands

Methodologies Used

The concept of economic value of environmental resources such as ecosystems is anthropocentric in nature. The economic valuation of environmental resources such as wetlands is concerned ultimately with the allocation of wetland resources to improve human welfare.

For the computation of the total economic value of wetland ecosystems it is helpful to classify wetland values into:

(i) direct use values: the values derived from the direct use or interacting with wetlands resources and services.

(ii) indirect use values : the values derived from the indirect support and protection provided to an economic activity and property by the natural ecological functions of wetlands.

(iii) Option and quasi-option value: the values based upon the future demand of a particular resource

(iv) Non-use values: current and future (potential) values associated with an environmental resource which rely merely on its continued existence and are unrelated to its current use. (Pearce and Warford, 1993)

As has been explained elsewhere, wetlands provide a host of goods and services. Based upon the classification of use and nonuse values the total economic valuation framework for wetlands is worked out (Barbier (1994), Scodari (1990)) and is given in Table 1.

Direct use values of wetlands consist of familiar activities like fishing, fuelwood and fodder extraction and agriculture. These activities can be commercial or non-commercial in nature. Fishing, fuelwood or fodder collection for commercial purposes is easy to value because the end product enters the conventional market and thus has an economic value. Non-commercial direct uses of wetlands are often neglected but it is these that are critical in determining the economic value of tropical wetlands in developing countries. The failure to take this value into account is often a major factor behind policy decisions that lead to over exploitation or excessive degradation of tropical wetlands (Barbier, 1993).

Table 1: Framework for the economic valuation of use and nonuse values of wetlands

Use Values		Non-Use Values	
Direct Use Value	IndirectUse Value	Option and Quasi-option Value	Existence value
Fish	Nutrient retention	Potential future uses	Biodiversity
Agriculture	Flood control	Future value of information	Culture, heritage
Fuelwood	Storm protection		Bequest value
Recreation	Ground water recharge		
Transport	External ecosystem support		
Wildlife harvesting	Micro-climate stabilization		
	Shoreline stabilization		

Ecological functions performed by the wetlands have indirect use values because these functions support or protect economic activities that have direct measurable values. The indirect use values of ecological functions is related to the change in the value of production or consumption of activity or property that it is protecting (Barbier *et.al.*, 1997). For example, ground water recharge which occurs through the floodplains leading to the augmentation of the ground water reserve of the area. The volume of ground water, which is recharged through the floodplains, can be used for domestic, agricultural or industrial uses. Any change in the ground water reserve due to disruption of ground water recharge will lead to increased cost of acquisition of water for any of these activities resulting in welfare loss which can be estimated in economic terms. A special category of value is option value, which arises because an individual may be uncertain about his future demand for a resource and or its availability in the wetland in the future.

The total economic value of wetland ecosystem is estimated after the various use and non-use values are monetised. It is imperative that suitable economic valuation methodologies are used so as to get the most appropriate economic value for a particular good or service provided by the wetlands which reflects the importance of that good or service to the society.

Monetization of direct use values of wetlands is relatively simple because the end products can be assigned absolute value as they enter the conventional market. The major challenge is in assigning economic value to indirect use value of wetlands which comprise majorly of non market goods and services.

Studies have been carried out to capture the economic value of wetlands considering different ecological functions varying on a case to case basis. A few examples of economic valuation studies carried out across the world for assigning economic value to direct, indirect and option values of wetlands provide the basis for understanding the advantages and limitation of valuation of ecosystems in general and wetlands in particular and the role of natural resource accounting in achieving conservation and sustainable utilization of ecosystem resources.

Farber and Costanza (1987) estimated economic value of three primary contributions of coastal wetlands of Louisiana: commercial fishing and trapping, recreation and storm protection. Economic valuation was carried out using indirect (WTP) and energy analysis methods. Economic estimates of wetland services varied from 590 USD/acre using WTP to 6400-10600 USD/acre using Energy analysis method. 590 USD/acre represents the lower bound estimate because it excludes many wetland services and 6400-10600 USD/acre energy analysis estimates are high because they include wetland services which are not economically valuable. In Thailand, a combination of shrimp farming and sustainable yield forestry represents an output of 160-500 USD/ha/year (Dixon, 1989). The value of wetlands as nutrient sink was estimated for Stockholm archipelago. The value of wetlands corresponded to 430 USD/ha/year (Gren, 1993). In a study carried out in the Hadejia-Nguru wetlands in northern Nigeria the role of ground water recharge function of the floodplains in supporting dry season agriculture was investigated using the production function approach (Acharya, and Barbier, 2000). This study made explicit the crucial role which ground water recharge plays in the dry season agriculture being practiced by the local communities. It also highlighted loss of welfare which will result if there is disruption of this crucial ecological function.

In a multiinstitutional interdisciplinary study carried out by Centre for Environmental Management of Degraded Ecosystems, University of Delhi, Department of Business Economics, University of Delhi and Institute of Economic Growth an attempt was made to quantify the goods and services provided by the wetland ecosystems of Yamuna river corridor in Delhi region (Anonymous, 2001). In this study, four ecological functions performed by the wetland ecosystems were economically valued: (i) hydrological functions, (ii) biological productivity, (iii) nutrient storage and (iv) habitat for flora and fauna. The major focus of this study was to assess relative economic merits of conservation of wetlands ecosystems of Yamuna river corridor versus channelization of the river in the Delhi stretch for development of civic infrastructure including making river front resorts. For this a host of ecological and economic methodologies were used which included the use of water balance method, contingent valuation method and production function approach. The cost benefit analysis using different discount rates suggested that preservation of wetland ecosystems is economically more sound option as compared to the development of river front resorts.

Scope and Limitation of Valuation

Typical valuation studies take into account few or single value of wetlands from the myriad of values wetlands provide on a local, regional and global scale. This means that economic estimates arrived at in different valuation studies are lower bench mark values of wetland resources. Even then these economic estimates prove that wetlands are highly productive economic resources and conversion of wetlands for alternative development options represent inefficient resource use.

Economic values are assigned to incremental changes which occur in the ecological function being valued; this principle works best when increments are small and the change in the ecological function has minimal feedback on the rest of the system. Ecosystems being highly interdependent systems and the change in a single ecological function can lead to a cascading effect on other ecological functions of the ecosystem. Moreover, segregation and classification of ecological functions of wetlands into discrete values is done for ease of analysis ignoring the extensive interconnections present among various functions. Economic valuation studies carried out to monetize ecological functions ignore this very important characteristic of ecosystems.

Use of a specific valuation technique depends upon the nature of ecological function, data availability on various ecological and economic parameters and the time period for which the analysis is carried out. Any valuation technique works under certain simplifying assumptions of the system. Therefore, conclusions and assumptions drawn on the basis of economic estimates should be treated with caution. For example contingent valuation method, used for estimating non-market goods and services, is highly unreliable particularly when it is used for the estimation of willingness to pay from the general public who are not familiar with the particular good or service being valued.

Ecological processes which regulate ecosystem function such as:(i) natural thresholds of ecosystems in which they generate flow of ecosystem services, and (ii) role of disturbance regimes in ecosystem functioning are not clearly understood in ecological science consequently the importance of economic valuation is questionable. Moreover, it is difficult to put economic value on attributes of ecosystems such as the resilience of natural ecosystems to exogenous and endogenous perturbations.

Conclusion

Though there are many limitations of economic valuation of ecosystems, natural resource accounting provides a tool in the hands of policy makers and planners to arrive at a rational decision with regard to conservation of natural ecosystems. Tools and techniques of natural resource accounting provide methodology by way of which the crucial role of many non-market goods and services provided by the ecosystems in the development of human society can be made explicit. To develop strategies for sustainable utilization of ecosystems services a more robust understanding is required with respect to the ecological processes that regulate ecosystems with further development of more effective economic valuation techniques. To make natural resource accounting more practical and meaningful, we must look for meaningful ecological and economic indicators which reflect ecosystem health and economic development. Finally, ecological security and economic development can only be assured when ecological theory is integrated with economic theory.

References

Anonymous, 2001. *Valuation of Ecological Functions and Benefits:* A Case Study of Wetland Ecosystems Along the Yamuna River Corridors of Delhi Region (P-198) undertaken by Centre for Environmental Management of Degraded Ecosystems and Department of Business Economics, University of Delhi, Institute of Economic Growth. The Indira Gandhi Institute of Development Research, Mumbai.

Acharya, G. and Barbier, E.B., (2000). Valuing ground water recharge through agricultural production in the Hadejia-Nguru wetlands in northern Nigeria. *Agricultural Economics,* 22:247-259

Barbier, E.B., (1993). Sustainable use of wetlands valuing tropical wetland benefits: economic methodologies and appiications. *The Geographical Journal,* 159 (1): 22-32

Barbier, E.B., (1994). Valuing environmental functions: tropical wetlands. *Land Economics,* 70 (2): 155-73

Barbier, E.B., Acreman, M. and Knowler, D., (1997). *Economic Valuation of Wetlands,* Ramsar Convention Bureau, IUCN

Dixon, J.A., 1989. Valuation of mangroves, *Tropical Coastal Area Management,* 4: 1-6

Farber, S. and Costanza, R., (1987). The economic value of wetlands ecosystem, *Journal of Environmental Management,* 24: 41-51

Gren, I-M., 1993. Alternative nitrogen policies in the Malar region, *Ecological Economics* 7: 159-172

Pearce, D.W. and Wraford, J.J., (1993). *World Without End,* Oxford University Press, Oxford

Scodari, P.F., (1990). Wetlands protection: the role of economics, *Environmental Law Institute Monograph,* Washington, D.C.

Turner, R.K., (1991). Economics and wetland management. *Ambio,* 20 (2): 59-63

UNEP, (1992). United Nations Environment Programme, Status of Biodiversity, Cambridge University Press.

WCMC, (1992). World Conservation and Monitoring Centre, *Global Biodiversity: Status of the Earths Living Resources,* Chapman and Hall, London.